Journal of Semitic Studies Supplement 38

The Formation of Quadriliteral Verbs in Iraqi Arabic Dialects

by

Sadok Masliyah

Published by Oxford University Press
on behalf of the University of Manchester
2017

OXFORD
UNIVERSITY PRESS

Great Clarendon Street, Oxford OX2 6DP

Oxford University Press is a department of the University of Oxford.
It furthers the University's objective of excellence in research, scholarship,
and education by publishing worldwide in

Oxford New York

Athens Auckland Bangkok Bogotá Buenos Aires Cape Town
Chennai Dar es Salaam Delhi Florence Hong Kong Istanbul Karachi
Kolkata Kuala Lumpur Madrid Melbourne Mexico City Mumbai Nairobi
Paris São Paulo Shanghai Singapore Taipei Tokyo Toronto Warsaw

with associated companies in Berlin Ibadan

Published in the United Kingdom
by Oxford University Press, Oxford

First published 2017

A catalogue for this book is available from the British Library

Library of Congress Cataloguing in Publication Data
(Data available)

ISSN 0022-4480
ISBN 978-0-19-881669-0

Subscription information for the *Journal of Semitic Studies* is available at the journal website:
jss.oxfordjournals.org

Printed in Great Britain by Bell & Bain Ltd, Glasgow

Table of Contents

General Description v

Transcription Scheme vi

A. Reproduction of Biliteral Verbs and Two Consonants of the Triliteral Verbs Internally 1

A. 1. Type 1.2.1.2 1

A. 2. Type 1.2.3.2 5

A. 3. Type 1.2.3.3 6

A. 4. Type 1.2.1.4 6

A. 5. Type 1.1.3.4 8

B. Augmentation of Triradical Verbs Externally by Attaching 1. Prefixes, 2. Infixes, 3. Suffixes 9

B. 1. Prefixes

B. 1.1. Type '. 2.3.4 9

B. 1.2. Quadriradical Verbs Type H or '. 2. 3. 4 10

B. 1.3. Type Sh. 2.3.4 11

B. 1.4. Type S. 2.3.4 13

B. 1.5. Type M. 2.3.4. 13

B. 1.6. Type, T, Ṭ. 2.3.4 16

B. 1.7. Type B, or D, Ḥ, L, 2.3.4 17

B. 2. Quadriradical Verbs Resulting from Triradical Verbs Augmented by an Infix after the First Radical of the Triliteral Verb 19

B. 2.1. Type 1. R. 3.4 19

B. 2.2. Type 1. N. 3.4 23

B. 2.3. Type 1. W. 3.4 27

B. 2.5. Type 1. ', or B, L, M, H, N, R, T. 3.4 34

B. 2. Quadriradical Verbs Resulting from Triradical Verbs Augmented Externally by Adding an Infix after the Second Radical of Triliteral Verbs 37

B. 2.6. Type 1.2. M. 4 37

B. 2.7. Type. 1.2 .W. 4 37

B. 2.8. Type 1.2. B, L, R, T, Ṭ, '. 4 40

B. 3. Augmentation of Triradical Verbs Externally by Adding Suffixes 43
B. 3.1. Type 1.2. 3. M 43
B. 3.2. Type 1.2.3. N 43
B. 3.3. Type 1.2.3. L 45
B. 3.4. Type 1.2.3. Sh 46
B. 3.5. Type 1.2.3. S 47
B. 3.6. Type 1.2.3. ʿ 47
B. 3.7. Type 1.2.3. R 47
B. 3.8. Type 1.2.3. B 48
B. 3.9. Type 1.2.3.T or Ṭ (but some are not suffixes) 48
C. 3. Deriving Quadriliteral Verbs by Procedures other than by A or B above: 1. Denominatives, 2. Composition and Blends 49
C.3.1. Denominatives 49
C. 3.2. Quadriradical Verbs Resulting from Composition (*Naḥt*) and Blends 54
D. Borrowing from other Semitic Languages and Non-Semitic Languages: Persian, Turkish, English, French, Italian and Greek 57
D.1.1. Turkish and Persian 57
D.1.2. English 61
D.1.2. French 62
D.1.2. Italian 62
D.1.2. Greek 63
APPENDIX I: Verbs Type 1.2.1.2 65
APPENDIX II: Type 1.2.1.4 83
APPENDIX III: Denominatives 89
REFERENCES 101

General Description

One of the major structural characteristics of all Semitic languages is the root system. Most Semitic verb roots are triradicals and Arabic is no exception. However, Arabic and other Semitic roots may also be bi-radicals and quadriradical verbs. The purpose of this study is to investigate quadriradical verbs in spoken Iraqi Arabic (IA, hereafter) and explore the procedures for their formation. I have gathered the basic materials from Iraqi spoken-Arabic dictionaries, Iraqi folk songs, proverbs, tales and poetry, as well as from several sources on other Arabic dialects, and consulted three natives from different parts of Iraq. Comparisons with Classical Arabic (CA, hereafter), Persian, Turkish, Hebrew, Aramaic, Syriac and a few European languages are used to substantiate the meaning of these verbs. Although there is no guarantee that all these quadriliteral verbs remain in use, it illustrates a principle, a procedure, or a tendency in the creation of such verbs.

Participles may be considered as part of a verbal system because of their syntactical functions and semantic meanings; hence I also have included participles that are not actually attested in every-day interactions.

The quadriliteral verbs in Arabic established a system, which compared to the triradical verbs, add a new dimension and flexibility to speakers of Arabic and facilitates meeting the increasing daily demands of the modern era for new modes of expression. The basic function of the expansion into quadriradical verbs is to indicate intensity or repetition of the ideas denoted by the triradical or the bi-radical verbs.

Qadriliteral verbs are largely a result of the duplication of bi-consonant verbs, adding prefixes, infixes and suffixes to the triliteral verb, as well as other procedures that serve for deriving verbs from nouns and other parts of speech. These procedures are common in all Semitic languages.[1] The duplication of bi-consonant verbs comprises the largest group of quadriradical verbs in Arabic.

It should be mentioned that there are ethnic and geographical differences among the socio-religious communities of Iraq. The Christians and the Jews of Baghdad speak dialects different from that of the Muslims, and the Jews mix certain Turkish, Persian, Aramaic and Hebrew lexical items in their everyday speech. Additionally, the rural sedentary dialect differs from the urban Muslim dialect of Baghdad and some other

1 S. Moscati et al., *An Introduction to the Grammar of the Semitic Languages* (Wiesbaden 1980), 84 (henceforth Moscati).

cities. Dialectal differences also exist within Baghdad, due to classification and a continuous flow of a greater number of non-Baghdadi speakers into the city.[2]

There are many quadriliteral verbs in this study that are mentioned in the sources without meanings and seem to have more than one possible procedure or stem. I have tried to explore the meanings of these verbs and procedures and to sort them into their categories. The following shows the characteristic procedures and the meanings of a considerable number of quadriradical verbs in IA. For convenience, I have classified the data under the following headings:

A. Reproduction of Biliteral Verbs and Two Consonants of the Triliteral Verbs Internally.

B. Augmentation of Triradical Verbs Externally by Attaching:
 1. Prefixes, 2. Infixes, 3, Suffixes.

C. Deriving Quadriliteral Verbs by Procedures Other than from A or B above:
 1. Denominatives, 2. Composition (*Naḥt*) and Blends.

D. Borrowing from Other Semitic Languages and Non-Semitic Languages: Persian, Turkish, English, French, Italian and Greek.

Transcription Scheme

The transcription scheme adopted in this study is as follows:

The use of /'/as a symbol of the glottal stop initial position is dropped unless it is followed by a long vowel.

The sound /çi/, a voiceless palatal affricative, is similar to the first sound of the English word *church*.

Pausal *tā' marbūṭah* is used when reference is made to Classical Arabic (CA), but omitted in Iraqi Arabic (IA) unless it is changed to /t̠/ due to suffixing or *iḍāfah*, (*qal'ah-qal'atuhu, qal'at Ṣāliḥ*).

/l/ stands for voiced alveo-dental lateral, velarized, similar to English *l* in *mill*.

/gh/ is the transcription of the voiced velar spirant, similar to French *r*.

/dh/ is the voiced interdental spirant, similar to the English *th* as in *than*.

The voiceless glottal spirant similar to the English *h* in *home* is transcribed as /h̲/.

The voiceless interdental spirant similar to the English *th* as in *thank* is /th/.

2 H. Blanc, *Communal Dialects in Baghdad* (Cambridge 1964), 182, and S. Altoma, *The Problem of Diglossia in Arabic: A Comparative Study* (Cambridge 1969), 6 (henceforth Altoma).

/ḍ/ is the voiceless interdental, spirant, velarized (no equivalent in English).

Other Arabic sounds that have no equivalent in English are transcribed as follows:

/q/ is a voiceless uvular stop.

/ʿ/ is a voiced pharyngeal spirant.

/ṭ/ stands for dental stop, velarized.

/ṣ/ stands for the voiceless dental spirant, velarized.

The voiceless pharyngeal spirant and the voiceless velar spirant (similar to German *ch* in *Bach*) are transcribed as /kh/ and /ḥ/respectively.

In Iraqi Arabic (IA), the sound /ẓ/ merges with /ḍ/.

The definite article is transcribed as *al* regardless of whether it is attached to a word beginning with a sun or a moon letter.

Short and long vowels are transcribed as a/ā, i/ī, u/ū and o/ō.

/ā/stands also for *yā' maqṣūrah* which ends quadriliteral verbs.

The sound of the vowel in /face/ is transcribed as /é/.

The first sound in /oval/ is transcribed as /ō/.

The contrast e̲:i̲ noted for some speakers of IA is ignored here.

No attempt is made to indicate stress since in the majority of cases it falls on the first vowel of words having two syllables, otherwise it is placed on the vowel which precedes the last V or CC.

Finally, the symbol √ denotes a grammatical root (the radicals are always capitalized).

The abbreviations of the references are: IA= Iraqi Arabic, CA = Classical Arabic, Arm = Aramaic, Syr = Syriac, Akk = Akkadian, Kur = Kurdish, Per = Persian, Tur = Modern Turkish, OTurk = Ottoman Turkish, Ita = Italian, Fr = French, Eng = English and Gr = Greek. The references in the text are either abbreviated (see References) or mentioned by the last name of the author and the first word of her/his work.

A. Reproduction of Biliteral Verbs and Two Consonants of the Triliteral Verbs Internally

A. 1. Type 1.2.1.2[3]

A considerable number of verb types (1.2.1.2.) in IA are onomatopoetic, i.e. verbs that imitate the sounds in nature or of animals and objects. Some of them are borrowed. This feature exists in all the other Semitic languages (Kāmil, 22). Examples of such verbs in IA (and CA) are *waṣwaṣ*, 'to twitter', (Mac, I, 415[4]; Ḥana, *al-Alfāẓ*, 391[5]; Bak, 495[6]; Cha, *Ath*, 87[7]) < Arm, *ṣwāṣ*, 'twitter'; 'to peep', (Gīl, 278[8]); 'to bark'; (Bak, 34) and figuratively, 'to complain'; *mawmaw*, 'to meow', ('Awwād, 22[9]); 'to neigh'; 'to clear one's throat', (Mac, I, 418); *qarqar*, 'to grumble' (hen), (Sām, 197[10]), as in *baṭnī datqarqir jū'ān*, 'my stomach is growling, I am hungry', (Wood, 371[11]); *ja'ja'*, 'to scream' < Syr, *j'āthā*, 'loud scream', Arm, (Cha, *Ath*, 125), and figuratively, 'to long for', (FM, 101[12]).

---

3 See examples of this type of quadriliteral verbs in some other Arabic dialects, Murād Kāmil, *Nash'at al-Fi'l al-Rubā'ī fī al-Lughāt al-Sāmiyyah al-Ḥayyah* (Cairo 1963), 80–6 (henceforth Kāmil); G.R. Driver, *A Grammar of Colloquial Arabic of Syria and Palestine* (London 1925), 77 (henceforth Driver); Yosėf Ṭobī, 'ha-Pe'alīm ha-Meruba'īm ba-'Ivrīt ha-Meduberet shebėfi Yehuday Ṣan'a', (Hebrew), *Masorot* II (1986), 65–78, p. 70 (henceforth Ṭobī); Moshe Piamenta, *A Dictionary of Post-Classical Arabic* (2 vols. Leiden 1990), I: 20, 38, 42, 56, 152, 218, II: 278, 301, 349 (henceforth Piamenta). There are many examples of this type of quadriliteral verbs in the Lebanese dialect cited in Anīs Furayḥah's *Mu'jam al-Alfāẓ al-'Āmmiyyah*, (Beirut 1973) (henceforth AF, *Mu'jam*). The most comprehensive work on quadriradical verbs in Arabic is Kāmil's *Nash'at al-Fi'l al-Rubā'*, pp. 1–25 in Arabic. A non-Arabic part is in German, French, English, and Italian in which the author presents quadriliteral verbs in nine Arabic dialects including two dialects spoken in southern Arabia, five in Ethiopia, and two Neo-Aramaic. Both Ibrāhīm al-Sāmarrā'ī's work, *al-Fi'l Zamānuhu wa-Abniyatuhu* and MacCarthy's two volumes, *Spoken Arabic of Baghdad*, devote chapters to quadriliteral verbs in Iraqi Arabic. Kūrkīs 'Awwād's *Ashtāt Lughawiyyah* (Beirut 1990) lists 492 such verbs in IA, but without mentioning their meanings.

4 R. MacCarthy and F. Raffouli, *Spoken Arabic of Baghdad* I (Baghdad 1964), (henceforth Mac, I).

5 Jalāl al-Dīn al-Ḥanafī, *Mu'jam al-Alfāẓ al-Kuwaytiyyah* (Baghdad 1964), (henceforth Ḥana, *al-Alfāẓ*).

6 Ḥāzim al-Bakrī, *Dirāsāt fī al-Alfāẓ al-'Āmmiyyah al-Mawṣūliyyah*, (Baghdad 1972), (henceforth Bak).

7 Dawūd al-Çalabī, *al-'Āthār al-'Ārāmiyyah fī Lughat Mawṣul al-'Āmmiyyah* (Baghdad 1935), (henceforth Cha, *Ath*)

8 Gīlaḥ Swėry and R. Rajwān, *Dictionary of Iraqi Judeo-Arabic Dialect*, (in Hebrew) (Jerusalem 1995), 278 (henceforth Gīl).

9 Kūrkīs 'Awwād, *Ashtāt Lughawiyyah*, 22 (henceforth 'Awwād).

10 Ibrāhīm al-Sāmurrā'ī, *al-Fi'l Zamānuhu wa-Abniyatuhu* (Baghdad 1966), (henceforth Sām).

11 D. Woodhead and B. Wayne, *A Dictionary of Iraqi Arabic, Arabic-English* (Washington 1967), (henceforth Wood).

12 Fāḍīl Mubāraka, *Baqāyā al-'Ārāmiyyah fī Lughat Ahl Ṣadad al-Maḥkiyyah* (Aleppo 1990), (henceforth FM).

Examples of quadriradical verbs resulting from sounds made by objects are *jazajaz*, 'to squeak', 'to make the sound *jaz jaz*, when walking in new shoes', *taktak*, 'to make the sound *tak tak* in an invariable rhythm' (clock), *la'la'*, 'to boom', (Mac, I, 418) < Arm, *méla'lō'e*, (Ben-Jacob, *Hebrew and Aramaic*, 97[13]) < Heb, *lō-a'*, 'throat', Heb, *la'ah*, 'to stutter'.

Other types of 1.2.1.2, verbs may denote the following:

a. Defects in pronunciation like *tamtam*, ('Awwād, 23); 'to stutter', *ta'ta'*, 'to mumble with fright', *fa'fa'*, 'to stammer', 'to repeat the sound /f/', CA, 'same'.
b. Repetitions of biliteral verbs denoting intensity of action. Examples of such verbs are: *sadsad*, 'to bolt', 'to fasten well', 'to close firmly', (Mac, I, 418) < *sadda*, 'to close'; *fajfaj*, 'to split in many pieces' < *fajja*, CA, 'to slice', 'to straddle'; *lamlam*, 'to gather, collect pieces', (Mac, II, 531[14]; Ḥajj IV, 279[15]) < *lamma*, 'to gather', CA, 'same', Arm, *mélamlomé*, (YM I, *Hebrew-Aramaic*, 264[16]); *zalzal*, 'to quake' (earth), 'to cause to tremble' < *zalla*, 'to slip', (al-Karmilī, *Majmū'ah*, I, 191[17]); *ṭakhṭakh*, 'to shake one's buttock'; *ṭakhkh*, 'to collide', 'to bump', (Wood, 287; Mac, II, 440), *takhtakh*, ('Awwād, 23), *takhkh*, 'to become wet, or soft, or fermented', (Ḥana, *Mu'jam*, II, 41[18]), 'to be overwhelmed', as in the expressions *min shāf jamālhā takhtakh*, 'whoever sees her beauty will be stunned', and *idhā trīd itakhtikhhā inṭīhā mashrūb*, 'if you want to weaken [her resistance] give her a drink', (Wood, 55).
c. There are, however, very few verbs of the type 1.2.1.2, which denote a lesser action than the bi-radical verb: *rafraf* (Bak, 291), 'to open and close the eyelids'; 'to flutter', (Mac, I, 415), CA, *raffa*, CA, *méraprōpéh*, Arm (YM I, *Hebrew-Aramaic*, 291), *rashrash*, 'to sprinkle a little', *rashsh*, 'to sprinkle', (Wood, 188).
d. Repetition offers no additional connotation, except perhaps that the expanded form was felt to be phonetically more expressive than the regular bi-radical form as in

13 A. Ben-Jacob, *Hebrew and Aramaic in the Language of the Jews of Iraq* (Hebrew), (Jerusalem 1985), (henceforth Ben-Jacob, *Hebrew and Aramaic*)

14 R. MacCarthy and F. Raffouli, *Spoken Arabic of Baghdad* II (Baghdad 1967), (henceforth Mac, II).

15 'Azīz al-Ḥajjiyyah, *Baghdādiyyāt* IV (Baghdad, 1981), (henceforth Ḥajj IV).

16 Mordechai Yona, *Hebrew-Aramaic-Kurdish Dictionary* (Hebrew] (Jerusalem 1990), (henceforth YM I, *Hebrew-Aramaic*).

17 Anastas Mārī al-Karmilī, *Majmū'ah fī al-Aghānī al-'Irāqiyyah*, 2 Vols, (Amīr al-Sāmarrā'ī [ed.], Baghdad 1999), (henceforth al-Karmilī, *Majmū'ah*).

18 Jalāl al-Dīn al-Ḥanafī, *Mu'jam al-Lughah al-'Āmmiyyah al-'Irāqiyyah* II (Baghdad 1982), (henceforth Ḥana, *Mu'jam*, II).

washwash, 'to whisper', (Mac, I, 410 415; DH, *Qāmūs*, 301) < *washsh*, IA, *'iwshé'ash*, Arm, 'light noise', (Bak, 495).

e. Quadriradical verbs type 1.2.1.2. may also be a result of reproduction of two consonants of the weak triradical verbs, mostly of verbs whose second or third radical is a glide *wāw* or *yā'*. When a quadriradical verb is derived from such verbs, the *wāw* or *yā'* is deleted and the remaining two radicals are duplicated. Examples include *bikā*, 'to weep', *bakbak* and *baçbaç*, 'to cry a lot, pleading', Arm, *mébakbokéh*, (YM I, *Hebrew-Aramaic*, 187); 'to cry continuously', (Bak, 12); *sa'sa'*, 'to make a living', *sa'ā*, 'to endeavour', CA, √ S'Y, *saqsaq* (tr.) 'to wash with water' < *saqā*, 'to water', 'to drink' (intr.) √ SQY, *'aṣ'aṣ*, 'to be stuck', 'to become hard' < *'aṣṣa*, 'same', (Thin, 90[19]), *ja'ja' ja'ā*, CA, 'to bleat', 'to make the loud sound of an ox meeting a cow', metaphorically, 'to desire', 'to long for', (FM, 101) *khaskhas*, 'to become spoiled' (fruits, vegetables) < *khāsa*, CA, 'to become stagnant', √ KhYS, *dasdas*, 'to step on repeatedly' < *dāsa*, 'to press', 'to search', (Ḥana, *Mu'jam*, III, 52[20]), < *dōsah*, 'noise',√ DWS; *dashdash*, 'to tread a lot'< *dashsha*, 'to tread', CA, 'same' or < *dashīsh*, Akk, 'coarsely ground wheat',√ DWSh, Arm, *déyashah*, 'tramping', (YM I, *Hebrew-Aramaic*, 105; Sām, 197).

f. Some 1.2.1. 2. verbs originated from triliteral verbs with initial *nūn*. Examples: *ṭafṭaf*, 'to drip' < *naṭafa*, CA, Heb, *naṭaf*, 'same', Arm, *ṭapṭap*, (Cha, *Ath*, 64; Bak, 271; YD, *Sefat*, 197[21]), *qaṣqaṣ*, 'to cut to small pieces' < *naqaṣa*, 'to decrease', (Mez, 253),[22] *ṭaf ṭaf*, 'to make noise when walking wearing a long, wet dress', (Cha, *Ath*, 64; Bak, 324).

g. Several verbs of the type 1.2.1.2. in IA are derived from Arabic and non-Arabic denominatives, such as, *ma'ma'a*, 'to bleat', (Erwin, *A Short Reference*, 79) < *ma'ma'ah*, 'an uproar', CA. It occurs in the expression *yibla' wīma'mi'*, said sarcastically, 'he swallows and makes a sound like sheep' (said about a greedy person), *warwar*, 'to be in flames'< *warr*, Arm, 'fire', *wajwaj*, 'to burn' < *ajja*, CA, 'same', *murmuh*, 'to exasperate', (Wood, 437), 'to make s.th. bitter' (*murr*), 'to tantalize', (Mac, I, 411; Dabb, 95[23]; Cha, *Ath*, 82); *'ash'ash*, 'to build a nest', (Mac,

19 'Abd al-Laṭīf Thinyān, *Ṣafaḥāt min Qāmūs al-'Awām fī Dār al-Salām* (Baghdad 2001), (henceforth Thin).

20 Jalāl al-Dīn al-Ḥanafī, *Mu'jam al-Lughah al-'Āmmiyyah al-'Irāqiyyah* III (Baghdad 1993), (henceforth Ḥana, *Mu'jam*, III).

21 Yoséf Davīd, *Sfat ha'ém: Milon ha-Nistolgyah shél ha-'Iraqīm*, (Hebrew, n.d), (henceforth YD, *Sefat*).

22 For more examples, see A. Mez, *Uber einige sekundare Verba im Arabischen, Orientalische Studien, Th. Noldeke, I* (Giessen 1906), 253.

23 Salmān Dabbī, *Hāyī al-Qiṣṣah, Tā'ālū Isma'ūhā*, Vol. 1 (Shafā 'Amr, Israel 1990), (henceforth Dabb).

I, 415) < *'ishsh*, 'nest'; *laqlaq*, 'to lap', (Mac, I, 415); 'to talk a lot of nonsense', used as an epithet (Ḥajj, VII, 212[24]; Shāl, II, 605[25]; 160[26]); 'to flatter', (Ben-Jacob, *Hebrew and Aramaic*, 98); (Bak, 443 < CA, *laqlāq*, 'tongue'; Ḥana, *al-Alfāẓ*, 326).

h. There is a host of Aramaic and Hebrew quadriradical verbs in IA, most of which are used by Iraqi Jews and Christians in Mosul (Aramaic) and less in other cities of Iraq. These are important linguistic materials which exist in Judaeo-Arabic writings and in the oral communications of Iraqi Jews including the Bible, the *Mishnah*, (the first part of the Talmud), the *Gemara*, (the second and supplementary part of the Talmud), in the Jewish texts of Medieval times, and in the *Kabbalah* (Jewish Mysticism). Other Hebrew and Aramaic components exist in the documents and letters exchanged among the Jewish communities within Iraq and those outside it. The Hebrew component, however, has much more impact, relatively, on Iraqi Jews than Aramaic does, as it has been integrated into their daily interactions and religious writings. Examples of these lexical items are mentioned in this study when speaking about the quadriliteral verbs used by the Iraqi Jewish community in Iraq. Avīshūr notes three geographical Jewish dialects spoken by Iraqi Jews.[27] The first one was in Baghdad, spoken also in Basra and ʿAmārah in the south. The second dialect is that of Mosul and of the Jewish communities north of Mosul (Zakho, ʿAqrah, Irbīl, Mārdīn) and other small communities in the north where Jews spoke Arabic, Aramaic, Kurdish, Turkish and Persian. The third Jewish dialect was that of the Jewish community of ʿAnah in the west of Iraq, near the Syrian border, and of Hīt, which was previously an important Jewish religious centre. In each of these three areas, Jews spoke Arabic with each other in the *qeltu* dialect, rather than in the *geltu* Muslim dialect. However, lexical, morphological, and phonological differences existed among all the three dialects, (Avīshūr, 162–72[28]). Examples of such quadriliteral verbs are: *sakhsakh*, 'to cause a conflict, a dispute', Heb, *sikhsékh* (Gīl, 55; Ben-Jacob, *Hebrew and Aramaic*, 55); *daqdaq*, 'to be strict', 'to scrutinize', Heb, *diqdéq* (Ben-Jacob, *Hebrew and Aramaic*, 102; Gīl, 91; Cha, *Ath*, 41). It is also used to intensify the action of *daqqa*, 'to knock repeatedly', (Bak,

24 ʿAzīz al-Ḥajjiyyah, *Baghdādiyyāt*, VII (Baghdad 1999), (henceforth Ḥajj, VII).

25 ʿAbbūd al-Shāljī, *Mawsūʿat al-Kināyāt al-ʿĀmmiyyah al-Baghdādiyyah* Vol. II (Beirut 1982), (henceforth Shāl).

26 Rifʿat Bazargān, *Muʿjam al-Alfāẓ al-Dakhīlah fī al-Lahjah al-ʿIrāqiyyah* (Baghdad 2000), (henceforth Baz).

27 On the Jewish dialect in Baghdad, see J. Mansoor, *The Jewish Dialect of Baghdad* (Jerusalem 1991).

28 Y. Avīshūr, *ha-ʿIvrīt she-ba-ʿArvīt ha-Yehūdīt: ha-Markīv ha-ʿIvrī véha-Aramī shél kehīlot yéhūday ʿIrāk, Sūryah ʾu-Mitzrāyim* (Jerusalem, 2000–1), (henceforth Avīshūr).

222) < *dardaq*, 'same', CA; *galgal*, 'to make round', 'to roll', Heb, *gilgél* (Ben-Jacob, *Hebrew and Aramaic*, 36); 'to curl the hair', (Gīl, 59; YD, *Sefat*, 138) < *galgāl*, Heb, 'a wheel'; *gamgam*, 'to stutter', Heb, *gimgém* (Gīl, 37; Ben-Jacob, *Hebrew and Aramaic*, 37), *lakhlakh*, 'to make dirty', Heb, *likhlékh* (Ben-Jacob, *Hebrew and Aramaic*, 96); 'to hit', (Ḥana, *al-Alfāẓ*, 325); *za'za'*, 'to agitate', 'to shake', (Mac, I, 415.19; Wood, 203; Mac, I, 425); 'to tremble', 'to scare', 'to shock', (Ben-Jacob, *Hebrew and Aramaic*, 59; Heb, *zi'zé-a'*, 'same'; *tarjam*, 'to translate', interpret', (Wood, 56; Erwin, *A Short Reference*, 80; Ḥana, *Mu'jam*, II, 52). This verb is derived from the Akkadian noun *tergumanu*, 'interpreter', Arm, *targém*, Heb, *tirgém*, and English, 'dragoman'. It has been suggested that the root of this verb is √ RGM, 'to speak loudly', (Yannay, 203, n. 1[29]; *Muḥīṭ*, 2[30]); *qaṭragh*, 'to complain', 'to accuse', (Gīl, 176; Ben-Jacob, *Hebrew and Aramaic*, 176), Heb, *qiṭrég*, 'same'. This verb is borrowed from Syriac. For more 1.2.1.2 verbs, see Appendix I below.

A. 2. Type 1.2.3.2

Quadriradical verbs with the second radical repeated after the third one are rare in Semitic languages (Moscati, 69). This type exits mainly in Syrian, Amharic and all the Arabic dialects in Ethiopia (Kāmil, 23). In Hebrew, for example, it is established in three examples and from a descriptive point of view only (Yannay, 71). In IA we find only a few verbs of this type which exist in CA or are borrowed from Turkish, Aramaic, or Syriac. Examples: *'aṣmaṣ* ('Awwād, 24), CA, *'amaṣa*, Syr < *'maṣ*, 'to have tearful eyes due to the smell of smoke or from cutting onions'; *saglag*, 'to roam aimlessly', (YD, *Sefat*, 123; Gīl, 341), *qashwash*, 'to gather wood', 'to select the best', (Bak, 375); *'ashwash*, 'to become dim in sight', (DH, *Qāmūs*, 194) √ 'ShW; *qashmash*, 'to be wrinkled, dried' < *kshām*, Syr (FM, 453), *'aṣmaṣ*, 'to complicate matters', 'to become difficult to crack' < *'aṣmāṣ*, 'a tough nut to crack', (Thin, 90; Bak, 338); *gan'aṣ*, 'to be bad and not ripe' (fruits and vegetables), Arm, *gh'īṣā*, 'bad', (Cha, *Ath*, 84; Bak, 433); *dakmak*, 'to push hard' < *dakama*, CA, 'same'.

---

29 Igal Yannay, 'The Quadriliteral Verbs in the Hebrew Language', Ph.D. dissertation (University of California, Los Angeles 1970), (henceforth Yannay).

30 Buṭrus al-Bustānī, *Muḥīṭ al-Muḥīṭ* (Lebanon, 1977), (henceforth *Muḥīṭ*).

A. 3. Type 1.2.3.3

Another type of quadriradical verb is 1.2.3.3. where the third and fourth radicals are identical, provided that the root structure results from the repetition of the third radical and is of a previously triradical root. The repetition of the third radical may occur in a previous nominal state or when the verb is borrowed from other languages, or from Arabic. This type of reduplication is attested in Hebrew, Egyptian, Lebanese, Syrian and Yemenite dialects, (Kāmil, 24). I have recorded only the following verbs in IA: *bashlal*, 'to hamper', 'to confuse', (DH, *Qāmūs*, 42[31]), *baḥṣaṣa*, 'to cover with pebbles or gravel' (a road), (DH, *Qāmūs*, 36) < *ḥaṣṣaba*, CA, 'same'; *bahrar* > *bahara* as in *bahrar min il-thalij*, 'he was blinded by the snow', (DH, *Qāmūs*, 48); *taqṣaṣ 'an*, 'to examine a piece of news'; *khézaz*, Arm, 'to swindle', 'to lure' < *khazza*, CA, 'same', ('Awwād, 23; 'Ubaydī, 51[32]); *talfaf* < *talifa*, CA, 'to become spoiled'.

In the following verbs, the repetition of the third radical occurs in a previous nominal state or the verb is borrowed. For example, *ba'rar*, and *ba'ghagh*, (Gīl, 27; YD, *Sefat*, 110), 'to drop dung' (sheep, goats, camels), (Wood, 40) < *ba'rūr*, 'dung', and *bakhshash*, 'to give *bakhshīsh*, 'tip', 'gratitude', Per, *bakhshīsh*, Tur, *bahshīsh*, *zanzan*, 'to be effeminate', (Wood, 207), Per, *zan*, 'woman', (Cha, *Kalimāt*, 40[33]), *'tzanzan*, 'to indulge in fornication', √ ZNY.

A. 4. Type 1.2.1.4[34]

These are quadriradical verbs in which the first radical is repeated after the second radical. The formation under consideration expresses repetition of the verb's action and is a result of denomination, dissimilation of verbs in Form II or borrowing. It is found in all the spoken Arabic dialects (Kāmil, 23). However, O'Leary (O'Leary, 215[35]) claims that this type of quadriliteral verb is rare in Arabic, but his claim does not hold true as far as IA and CA are concerned. A considerable number of this type of verb feature *r* as the second radical.

The following verbs are a few examples of such quadriliteral verbs. More are cited in Appendix II.

---

31 Ḥalīm Dammūs, *Qāmūs al-'Awām* (Damascus 1923), (henceforth DH, *Qāmūs*).

32 Azhar al-'Ubaydī, *al-Mawṣul, Ayyām Zamān*, (Mosul 1989), (henceforth 'Ubay).

33 Dawūd al-Çalabī, *Kalimāt Fārisiyyah Must'amalah fī 'Āmmiyyat al-Mawṣul* [Baghdad 1960), (henceforth, Cha, *Kalimāt*).

34 For this type of verbs in some other Arabic dialects, see Kāmil, 73–5, 87–8.

35 D.D. O'Leary, *Comparative Grammar of the Semitic Languages* (London 1923), (henceforth O'Leary).

A. Reproduction of Biliteral Verbs and Two Consonants of the Triliteral Verbs Internally

Baghba', 'to scare', (Bak, 85; Gīl, 27), *tbaghba'*, 'to be afraid', (Cha, *Ath*, 26; Gīl, 35).

Barba', 'to flourish', 'to prosper', (Sām, 193; Ḥana, *Mu'jam*, I, 487[36]) < *raba'a*, CA, 'to become fertile in the spring', (Shāl, III, 237[37]), *itbarba'*, 'to be scared', and in the Jewish dialect, *itbaghba'*, 'to be scared', (CH, *Ath*, 24; YM II, *Aramaic-Kurdish*, 55).

Barbaṣ, 'to irrigate the land', Arm, *rbaṣ*, 'same', (Ch, *Ath*, 46), or *barraṣa*, 'to water', dissim. *-rr-* > *-rb-*. A distortion of this verb is *ṭarbaṣ* (DH, *Qāmūs*, 38; Thin, 73), 'to be annoyed'.

Barbash, 'to blink' (eyes), 'to become blurry' (eyes), (YD, *Sefat*, 60; Mac, 416), *ramasha*, *m* > *b*, and the *b* is a prefix, (Sām, 153).

Barṭal, 'to bribe', CA, 'same'.

Daghfal, 'to get rid of', (YD, *Sefat*, 159).

Dahwar and *dahdar*, 'to hurl', 'to topple', (Erwin, *A Short Reference*, 78; Mac, 316; Bak, 230; Wood, 167, 168), *dihidwānah*, 'slop'.

Falfaṭ, 'to make cry bitterly' (baby), Arm, 'to torment', *tfalfaṭ*, 'to cry a lot', (Ch, *Ath*, 26; Bak, 125; DH, *Qāmūs*, 232), Arm, *ithpalpaṭ*, 'to suffer', Syr, *frāṭ* (Kāmil, 75).

Farfas, *faghfaṣ*, 'to move in order to free o.s.', (Thin, 116); 'to rid o.s. from an action one did or from s.th. one said', (Bak, 369).

Farfash, 'to recover', 'to be refreshed and happy', Ḥana, *al-Alfāẓ*, 277 < *rafatha*, 'to be well off', where *th* > *sh* (Bak, 369), Arm, *frās*, *farasa* < Syr, *faratha*, 'to entertain'.

Garga', *qarqa'*, 'to become worn out and noisy like a wooden wagon' < *gargū'ah*, 'weak', (al-Karmilī, *Majmū'at*, II, 153); 'to thunder', (Wood, 388; Mac, I, 416); 'to rock', 'to knock', (Thin, 163); 'to squeak', (Ḥana, *Mu'jam*, II, 99); 'to make continuous noise' (Gīl, 250); *kōkā*, 'to shake while walking' (Basra), (Dul, 95 n. 1)[38]; 'to walk fast', (Thin, 153); 'to play a game to determine who plays the next one', (Dul, 95).

---

36 Jalāl al-Dīn al-Ḥanafī, *Mu'jam al-Lughah al-'Āmmiyyah al-'Irāqiyyah* I (Baghdad 1993), (henceforth Ḥana, *Mu'jam*, I).

37 'Abbūd al-Shāljī, *Mawsū'at al-Kināyāt al-'Āmmiyyah al-Baghdādiyyah* III (Cairo 1983), (henceforth Shāl, III).

38 For a few features of the spoken Arabic in Basra see 'Abd al-Laṭīf al-Dulayshī, *al-Al'āb al-Sha'biyyah fī al-Baṣra* (Baghdad 1968), I: 7–12 (henceforth Dul); Sām, 235–44; M. al-Mallāh, 'Nukāt wa-Gharā'ib Lughawiyyah', *Lughat al-'Arab* 6 (1928), 349–53 (henceforth al-Mallāh, 'Nukāt') and 'Abd al-Khāliq al-Dabbāgh, *Mu'jam Amthāl al-Mawṣul* (n.p. 1956), 8–16 (henceforth al-Dabbāgh).

a. *q* > *j*, *qādir*, 'able' > *jādir*; *qarīb*, 'near' > *jarīb*, but more commonly *q* > *g* and seldom *gh* > *q*, e.g. *gāl* for *qāl*, 'he said', *gāḍī* for *qāḍī*, *ghafūr*, 'forgiven' > *qafūr*, and *qém*, for *gém*, 'clouds'.

b. Rarely *q* > *k*, as in *maqtūl*, 'killed' > *maktūl* and *qabqāb*, 'wooden slipper' > *kabkāb*. Seldom, *q* changes to *g* and *ṭ* > *n*, as in *qā'id*, 'siting', *gādir*, *yi'ṭī*, 'he gives'> *yinṭī* and *'aṭiyyah*, 'a gift' > *niṭiyyah*. This

Ka'kar, (tr.), 'to destroy' (intr.) 'to collapse' (wall), (DH, *Qāmūs*, 237; Wood, 388).

Marmaḥ, 'to sully', 'to coat', 'to oil', (Ḥajj, *al-Amthāl*, 105) √ MRGh, where , *gh* > *ḥ*, Syr < *rmāḥ* (FM, 201).

Marmash, 'to exploit others', (Bak, 460); 'to devour meat' < *marasha*, CA, 'to eat with a voracious appetite', (Sām, 194).

Qarqaṭ, 'to nibble' < Arm, *qrāṭ*, 'same', (Cha, *Ath*, 70); *qarraṭa*, CA, 'to give a little' (in Basra), (Dul, 98), 'to chew', 'to squander', (Wood, 387), 'to tear into small pieces', (*Muḥīṭ*, 730), dissim. *-rr-* > *-rq-*.

Sharshaṭ, < *sharraṭa*, 'to tear in small pieces', (Kāmil, 75).

Ṭarṭa', 'to be worn out', (Ḥana, *al-Alfāẓ*, 132).

For more examples see Appendix II below.

A. 5. Type 1.1.3.4

This type of quadriliteral verb exists in the dialects of Jālā and Somalia, North Africa and in Syria (Kāmil, 23). The only verbs of this type that I found in IA are borrowed from other languages:

Shashban, 'to be a protector of s.o.', Arm < *shabīn* and *shawshabīnah*, 'co-sponsor', *shoshobīnah*, 'best man', (Soko, 196[39]).

Shashkhan, 'to lose consciousness', (Bak, 285; Cha, *Kalimāt*, 122; Kāmil, 42), 'to eject bullets' < *shishkhān*, 'a model of an old rifle', (Shāl, III, 366; Thin, 63).

Shashqal, 'to weigh', Arm, *shāqōlā*, 'same', (Cha, *Kalimāt*, 54).

change exists in Mosul and Baghdad too. In the south more than in the other parts of Basra, *j* > *y*, as in *dajājah*, 'hen' > *dayāyah*.

c. *k* > *ç*, as in *yikwī*, 'it burns' > *yiçwī* and *ḥarrik*, 'move!' (tr.) > *ḥarriç*!
dh > *ḍ*, as in *ydhūq* > *yḍūq*, 'he tastes', and *ḍrā'*, 'arm' for *dhrā'*.

d. The change of *gh* > *kh* exists in Basra, as well as in Mosul and Baghdad, e.g. *maghsūl*, 'washed' > *makhsūl*. Likewise, the interchange of the sibilants *z*, *s* and *ṣ* in those three cities is common *s* > *ṣ*, as in *saṭḥ*, 'rooftop' > *ṣaṭḥ*, *sakhī* > *ṣakhī*, *lāziq*, *lāṣiq*, and *lāsiq*, 'he is gluing'.

39 Michael Sokoloff, *A Dictionary of Judeo Aramaic* (Ramat-Gan 2003), (henceforth Soko).

B. Augmentation of Triradical Verbs Externally by Attaching: 1. Prefixes, 2. Infixes, 3. Suffixes

B. 1. Prefixes[40]

B. 1.1. Type '.2.3.4

The Semitic languages, including Arabic, present a series of stems with prefixes: '- or ', or *h*- or *s*- or *sh*-. They share a causative connotation. The Semitic causative stems from prefix morpheme *hamzah* and *h* appear in Amharic and Late Aramaic (O'Leary, 34). The CA causative Form IV which prefixes a *hamzah* morpheme to the basic stem has an Aramaic counterpart, the *af'él* and the Hebrew *hif'īl*.

The following quadriradical verbs in IA are derived by adding one of the said four causative prefixes of the Semitic languages to the triradical root (Moscati, 124). An *imālah* is noticed in the IA quadriliteral verbs whose initial radical is *wāw*. As a result, the *wāw* becomes the long vowel *o*. Examples:

'Ōhab, 'to allow' < *wahaba* , 'same', 'to forgive', (Ḥana, *Fiqh*, VI, 63–6, p. 25[41]).
'Ōshar, 'to sharpen' (teeth) < *washshara*, 'same', (al-Karmilī, *Majmū 'ah*, II, n. 32).
'Ō 'ad, 'to promise'< *wa 'ada* (DH, *Qāmūs*, 18, 19).
'Ōmā, 'to hint', 'to gesture', *wama 'a*, 'to wink', CA (Ḥana, *Fiqh*, 18; Erwin, *A Short Reference*, 79); 'to signal', (Wood, 504).
'Ōrad, 'to give water' < *warada*, 'to go to a water well', (Ḥana, *Fiqh*, 65).
Mōjal, 'to be afraid' < *wajala*; (Gīl, 254), 'same'.

The following IA verbs are expanded by predication of the causative *hamzah* to the triliteral verbs whose initial radical is not *wāw*:

Adman, 'to become addicted', (Wood, 165).
Adrak, as in *adrak 'alayya-l-waqt*, CA 'it's time for me to leave', (Wood, 117; Ḥana, *Fiqh*, 64).
Adhhal, 'to startle'< *dhahila*, 'to be alarmed', CA, *dhihal* (Wood, 176).

---

40 For prefixed quadriliteral verbs in other Arabic dialects, see Ṭobī, 71–3, Kāmil, Arabic part, pp. 14–15, 41–9, and non-Arabic part, pp. 27–30.

41 Jalāl al-Dīn al-Ḥanafī, *Fī Fiqh al-'Āmmiyyah al-Baghdādiyyah, al-Turāth al-Sha'bī*, VI (Baghdad 1975), (henceforth Ḥana, *Fiqh*).

Aḥlam, 'to dream', (Ḥana, *Fiqh*, 64; al-Karmilī, *Majmū' ah*, II, 11).

Ajban, 'to be afraid', (Ḥana, *Fiqh*, 65).

Akhbar, 'to tell, notify', (Ḥana, *Fiqh*, 64).

Akṭa', 'to make a contract' < *kaṭi'a*, 'to be contractually obligated'.

Alham, 'to inspire', *lahama*, CA (Ḥana, *Fiqh*, 65).

Amkan, 'to be possible', (Ḥana, *Fiqh*, 65).

An'am and *akram*, expressions of appreciation, '[May God] give [you] abundance and be generous' [to you].

Antaj, 'to produce', (Wood, 451).

Anzal, as in *ḥiçāhā bimā anzal*, 'he told it in detail', (Ḥana, *Fiqh*, 65).

Aqna', 'to convince', (Ḥana, *Fiqh*, 64).

Aqnaṭ, 'to be silent'< *qanaṭa*, CA.

Aqsam, 'to swear', (Wood, 372).

Arbak, 'to be entangled in an affair', *ribak*, 'same', IA, (Wood, 180).

Arfaq, 'to accompany', (Wood, 192), *rāfaqa*, CA, 'same'.

Argham, 'to compel', (Wood, 190).

Arshad, 'to guide, direct', (Wood, 188).

Arwaḥ, 'to have an offensive smell', (DH, *Qāmūs*, 15).

Ashfaq, 'to take pity', (Wood, 244).

Ashrak, 'to be a polytheist', (Ḥana, *Fiqh*, 65).

Aṭram, 'to knock out a tooth', (DH, *Qāmūs*, 18).

Awjab, 'to be necessary', (Ḥana, *Fiqh*, 65).

Ayfat, 'she became pretty' (Baghdadi Jews), Heb, *yafah*, 'pretty', (Avīshūr, 225).

Az'aj, 'to make mad', 'to annoy', (Ḥana, *Fiqh*, 64).

Az'al, 'to enrage', (DH, *Qāmūs*, 15).

Azman, 'to become chronic', (Wood, 206).

B. 1.2. Quadriradical verbs type h or '.2.3.4

There are only scant triradical verbs in IA which are prefixed with '. In CA, a few survivals of a causative *h* occur in *'araḥa* > *hārāḥa*, 'to give rest to'; *harāda*, 'to wish for'< *arāda*; *halqama*, 'to feed by mouth'< *alqama*; *'aṣfara*, 'to dye yellow' < *iṣfarra*, 'to become yellow', (O'Leary, 221).

The change of initial *hamzah* to *h* or ' appears with a modification of meaning in a few verbs in CA like *abhala*, 'to let somebody do whatever he/she pleases' and *'abhala*, 'to leave a camel unattended', (O'Leary, 223); *ha'lama* and *a'lama*, 'to inform', (Mez, 251), and *fashila* and *'afshala*, 'to twist and wrap'. This verb is attested in Syriac *fshāl*.

The prefixing of ʿ to verbs is called *'an'anah* in CA. The following are quadriliteral verbs in IA whose initial radical is the prefix '.

'Anfaq, (ʿAwwād, 24) 'to run out of s.th.' *nafaqa*, CA, 'same', but in IA *m'anfaq* means 'distained', one who is aware of dirt (Bak, 466).

'Anṭas, 'to be stubborn' (donkey), 'to become swollen from beating', (Wood, 325).

'Anṭaz, 'to kick' (donkey), < *naṭaza*, CA, 'to kick', 'to move one's hips while walking', (YD, *Sefat*, 227).

'Arbad, 'to shout or speak loud incoherently', 'to behave improperly', (Wood, 306; Sām, 171), usually when one is drunk (Mac, I, 421; Thin, 85).

Harbad, (Sām, 183; YD, *Sefat*, 161) where ' > *h*, see *'arbad*.

Hatlaf, 'to become shabby', *mhtalif*, 'untidy', (Sām, 183; al-Karmilī, *Majmū'ah* II: 379, n. 15), < *talifa*, 'to become worn out, spoiled'.

Harwal, 'to run slowly', CA, 'same', (Sām, 183).

In the following verb, the prefix *h* of the quadriradical verb *handam*, 'to dress up', 'to make neat', (Wood, 483) is Arabicized from the Persian noun *andām*, 'stature', which originally meant an arm used for measurement (Cha, *Ath*,75).

B. 1.3. Type Sh. 2.3.4

Quadriliteral verbs included in this type feature *sh* (and *s*) as their first radical stems from the prefix element *sh* of the old Semitic causative stem, and *af'ala*, CA, (Moscati, 79). In Aramaic, the *sh*-prefix has more or less survived, and in biblical Aramaic it is mentioned only in the book of Ezra (14:3 and 4:13), but it is fairly frequent in Hebrew and Amharic (O'Leary, 218). Both *sh* and *s* are used in deriving triradical verbs from geminated verbs, as attested in the following examples in CA: *shadafa* < *daffa*, *shanjana* < *janna*, *shuḥudhu* < *ḥudhudhu*, *shamaṭa* < *maṭṭa*, *sakana* < *kanna*, *sadala* < *dalla* (Kāmil, 11).

The following are IA quadriliteral verbs with *sh* as prefix morpheme to triliteral verbs. Some of these verbs, however, are borrowed from other languages, or derived from Arabic denominatives. They are:

Shaqlab and *çaqlab*, 'to roll down', (ʿUbaydī, 49; Mac, 421; Gīl, 146). It also exits in the dialects of Syria and Lebanon, (AF, *Mu'jam*, 97 and A. Furayḥah, 'al-Fiʿl al-Rubāʿī Aṣluhu wa-Nushū'uhu wa-Maʿānīhī', *al-Muqtaṭaf* [1973], 184–91 [henceforth AF, 'al-Fiʿl']), as *shaqlab* < *qalaba*, CA, 'to roll (tr.) from top to bottom', Arm, *shaqlaw*, √ QLW, and the *w* > *b*, (Cha, *Ath*, 58; Sām, 156; Ḥana, *Mu'jam*, II, 296), *çaqlunbah*, (name of a children's game in Iraq), (MM, 130[42]), *tçaqlab*, 'to tumble head over heels', (Mac, I, 435).

Sha'bath, 'to make disorder', 'to make a mess', (Wood, 242) < *'abatha bi*, CA, 'to abuse', *tsha'bath*, 'to cling', 'to adhere', 'to hold tightly', (Bak, 121; Wood, 242).

Sha'laq, 'to light' < Arm, *'laq*.

Sa'lak ('Awwād, 23), CA *'allaqa*, 'to hang', *q* > *k*, and the *s* is a prefix, (YD, *Sefat*, 203).

Sha'rab, 'to Arabize', semantically a denominative of *'arabī*.

Shabhar, 'to be proud', 'to boast', Old Syr, *bhar* (FM, 266); 'to erect the ears'.

Shabraq, Arm, *mabrōqéh*, 'to shine', (YM II, *Aramaic-Kurdish*, 219[43]); 'to squander', (DH, *Qāmūs*, 150); 'to put a fence between borders'< Syr, *frāq*, 'to leave' (tr.), 'to divorce', Arm, *shbāq*, (Mélaméd, 481[44]).

Shaḥlaf, 'to exchange', Syr, 'same' < CA, *shaḥlafa*, 'same', (Rabīn, 149[45]).

Shakhla', 'to take off', 'to slip off a garment' < *khala'a*, CA, 'to make s.o. *khalī'*, 'dissolute'.

Shalfaḥ, ('Awwād, 24), 'to expose s.th. or s.o. to cold air' < (*lafaḥa*), 'same'; 'to grow', Syr, *lfāḥ*, (FM, 295).

Shalghan, 'to become like a *shalghīn*' (a thick date syrup with knots), (DH, *Qāmūs*, 159), CA, 'same'.

Shalhab, 'to kindle' < Arm *shahawīthā*, Syr, *lhāb* (FM, 299). In the Lebanese dialect, *shalhūbah*, 'spark of fire', (AF, *Mu'jam*, 98), *luhab*, CA, 'a flame', (Wehr, 879[46]), accordingly, 'to suffer from heat', and 'become thirsty', (Rabīn, 152; Cha, *Ath*, 83).

Shalqaḥ, ('Awwād, 24), 'to throw o.s. on a seat or on the floor to rest', (AF, *Mu'jam*, 99), *tshalqaḥ*, 'to stretch one's arms and legs while laying down', (Bak, 122; FM, 295), Syr, *lqaḥ*.

---

42 Majīd Muḥammad, *Majma' al-Mu'allafāt wal-Alfāẓ al-Ajnabiyyah fī al-Lughah al-'Irāqiyyah al-Dārijah* (Baghdad 1990), (henceforth MM).

43 Mordechai Yona, *Aramaic–Kurdish–Hebrew Dictionary* II (Hebrew) (Jerusalem 1990), (henceforth YM II, *Aramaic-Kurdish*).

44 Ezra Mélaméd, *Aramaic-Hebrew-English Dictionary of the Babylonian Talmud* (Hebrew) (Jerusalem 2005), (henceforth Mélaméd).

45 Chaim Rabīn, 'The Nature and Origin of the Shafʿel in Hebrew and Aramaic', *Erétz-Yisrael*, IX, W.F. Albright volume, (Hebrew), 148–58, (henceforth Rabīn).

46 Hans Wehr, *A Dictionary of Modern Written Arabic*, J. Milton Cowan (ed.) (New York 1964), (henceforth Wehr).

Shambakh, 'to open the legs widely', (Ḥajj, V, 355, n. 31[47]).

Shaḥnaq, 'to cry loudly and bitterly', (Naqqāsh, *Nzūlah*, 273; Gīl, 123; YD, *Sefat*, 98) √ ShHQ (the *n* is an infix), or < *nahaqa*, 'to bray a lot', (DH, *Qāmūs*, 158; Bak, 22 √ NHQ), *tshanhaq*, 'to sigh over s.th.', (Cha, *Ath*, 26).

Sharkal, 'to entangle', 'to prevent s.o. from going', 'to expel', 'to go by foot', *rjāl*, Syr (FM, 277); 'to work in a hurry' ('Ubaydī, 54).

Shaghkal, *shargal*, 'to do a job in a hurry', Arm, *shargal*, 'to confuse', *ishtargal*, 'to be confused', (Cha, *Ath*, 56; 'Ubaydī, 54).

Sharqaṭ, 'to collect', (Kāmil, 30), Syr, *rqāṭ*, 'to cut branches off vine trees', (FM, 280); 'to flare' (fire), (DH, *Qāmūs*, 153). The *ṭ* is a suffix.

Shartaḥ, 'to eat until satisfied', 'to live with abundance', where ' > *ḥ* and the *sh* is a prefix, Arm (Rabīn 151). This verb exists in the Lebanese dialect with the same meaning, (AF, *Mu'jam*, 92). In CA, 'to wear worn out clothes', 'to be thrifty' (opposite meaning).

B. 1.4. Type S. 2.3.4

The *saf'al* form is attested in several Semitic languages, including Arabic, Ethiopic, Aramaic and especially in the dialect of southern Algeria (O'Leary, 218–19; Kāmil, 28–9). The causative *s* prefixed to triliteral verbs is a secondary development of the causative with *sh* as a prefix. Quadriliteral verbs in *saf'al* originated in CA from denominatives, verbs in Forms I, II, III, while some are loan words.
Quadriliteral verbs in *saf'al* are few in IA. Examples:

Sa'lak, 'to kindle', *ma'lōqéh* (YM I, *Hebrew-Aramaic*, 278; Cha, *Ath*, 83); 'to send away', (DH, *Qāmūs*,140).

Salgham, 'to control o.s.', 'to restrain'< *lijām*, CA, 'muzzle', figuratively, 'to speak logically' < Syr, *lghōm*, 'to muzzle a horse', (FM, 244), *lajama*, CA, 'to restrain', (the *s* is a prefix).

Sarkal, 'to expel' < Syr, *rgāl*, 'to go by foot', (FM, 236; DH, *Qāmūs*, 140) < *rakila*, CA, 'to kick'.

B. 1.5. Type M. 2.3.4

Most of the quadriradical verbs with initial *m* originated from denominatives and verbal nouns (*al-maṣdar al-mīmī*). The *m*-prefix is very productive in the formation of Arabic

47 'Azīz al-Ḥajjiyyah, *Baghdādiyyāt* V (Baghdad, 1983), (henceforth Ḥajj, V).

nouns. It serves to express a rich variety of meanings, especially in the formation of nouns of instrument, nouns of place, abstract nouns, verbal nouns and participles. It also prefixes to triradical verbs in various stems. In Neo-Aramaic, the quadriradical verbs are formed by prefixing *m* to the active and passive participles if the Aramaic verb is a sound one (Kāmil, 15). In IA, quadriradical verbs of this type mostly originated from nouns or participles prefixed to triliteral verbs in various stems, or they are borrowed from CA, or Aramaic or Syriac. Examples follow:

Ma'ras, this verb is attested in the Gulf Arabic dialects as well, 'to pay money jewellery, clothes' (usually to the bridegroom), (Qaf, 427) < *'irs*, 'wedding', *tma'ghas*, (Mosul), 'to make improper body movements' < *'ars*, 'pimp', (Bak, 132).

Mablad, ('Awwād, 25), 'to galvanize'< *labada*, CA.

Maḍḥak, *tmaḍḥak*, (from laughing stock), 'to mock', (Ḥana, *Mu'jam*, II, 112).

Maghlaṭ, 'to cheat', 'to mislead', (AF, *Mu'jam*, 139); 'to distort', 'to cover up', 'to obscure', (Wood, 423; Bak, 441); 'to mislead', (AF, *Mu'jam*, 162) < *maghlūṭ*, 'mistaken', Arm, *gélaṭah*, 'a mistake', (Cha, *Ath*, 86); 'to be misled', Arm, *maghlōṭéh*, (YM I, *Hebrew-Aramaic*, 223).

Maghwaj, 'to pamper', 'to flirt', (woman), (DH, *Qāmūs* 66; 'Ubaydī, 48), *tnaghwaj*, 'to become pampered, coquetted', dissim. of *ghannaja*, *-nn->-nw* (Thin, 247).

Mahzā, more commonly *tmahzā*, 'to scorn', (Ḥana, *Mu'jam*, II, 111).

Mal'ab, more commonly *tmal'ab*, 'to play', (al-Karmilī, *Majmū'ah*, II, 208, n. 58). It is attested in Eastern Arabic, 'to be amused', (Driver, 78).

Malmas, 'to touch and check' < *lamasa*, 'same', (Sām, 194).

Malṭkh, *'imlaṭṭakh*, 'stained', (Turj, 99[48]).

Mandal, *tmandal*, 'to walk slowly and haughtily', (Ḥana, *Mu'jam*, II, 115; MM, 334; Bak, 133). However, *mandal* (noun) is an 'odoriferous wood' (Cha, *Kalimāt*, 187), which was imported from China and used to relieve pain by inhaling its aromatic smoke when burning it. If so, this verb may mean, 'to inhale an aromatic smoke'.

Manṭaq, *tmanṭaq*, 'to make sounds of enjoying food by chewing and licking the lips', (Gīl, 42; YD, *Sefat*, 48) < *tamaṭṭaqa* (Bak, 132), 'to put on gridle' (there is no relationship between the meaning in CA and IA).

Maqlab, 'to turn upside down' < *qalaba*, CA, 'same'; 'to forfeit', 'to fabricate' *qalib*, IA, 'unreal', 'forfeit', (Bak, 393).

48 'Abbās Turjmān, *Malāmiḥ al-Lahjah al-Najafiyyah, Uṣūluhā wa-Adabuhā* (Beirut 2002), (henceforth Turj).

Maqlaj, 'to pamper', more common is *tmaqlaj*, 'to talk or walk in an unnatural manner' (Wood, 442); 'to coquette', 'to make movements of a pampered child', (Ḥana, *Mu'jam*, II, 113; Thin, 131; Shāl, II, 325; al-Karmilī, *Majmū'ah*, I, 144, n. 44) , 'to boast as if one is carrying a *qilij*' (sword), (Baghdad)[49]; *tmajlaq*, 'to have fun doing stupid actions', (Bak, 132; Sām, 182).

Mar'al, magh'al, 'to do careless work', (Gīl, 212; Cha, *Kalimāt*, 181); 'to roll in dust or mud', (Mac, I, 415; Bak, 466; 'Ubaydī, 54; Wood, 437). The Jews of Baghdad say *tmagh'al wiyyāha*, figuratively, 'he had sex with her' (lit. 'he rolled around in dust with her'), (Gīl, 250; YD, *Sefat*, 248).

Margaṣ, 'to mince', (Wood, 437) < *marqōzéh* (Arm, YM I, *Hebrew-Aramaic*, 302; Cha, *Ath*, 302), *tmargaṣ*, 'to move daintily', (Ḥana, *Mu'jam*, II, 111, *Mu'jam*, III, 202 [Baghdad 1993]; Ḥajj, *al-Amthāl*, 289), 'to pretend to dance', (Dul, 37); 'to jiggle', (Mac, II, 566).

Maḍyaq, tmaḍyaq, 'to behave like a pampered person when speaking and walking', (Bak, 132).

Maḥshaḥ, 'to insert s.th. in a narrow place', *ḥashaka*, 'to cram', 'to squeeze', (DH, *Qāmūs*, 88), 'to move burning wood with a *miḥshāk*' (tongs).

---

49 Some features of the Baghdadi dialect are:

gh > kh, ghisal > khisal, 'to wash'; *ightālūh > ikhtālūh*, 'he assassinated him'. Less commn *gh > kh*; *th > z*, *dayyūth* , 'pimp' > *dayyūz*; *th > ṣ*, *'uthmallī > 'uṣmallī*, 'Ottoman'; *th > t*, *nakatha*, 'to break a contract or a legal obligation' > *nakat*, *thalāthah > talātah*, 'three'.

q > g, wuqaf > wugaf, 'he stood', *quṭun > guṭun*, 'cotton'; *q > k, waqt > wakit*, 'time'; *qital > kital*, 'he killed'; *qoqā > kokā*, 'to grumble' (hen), 'captain' (Eng.) > *qabṭān*, but *q > gh* is rare, *laghlagh*, 'to talk a lot of nonsense', *laqlāq*, 'tongue'; *q > j, sharqī > sharjī*, 'northern'; *qadaḥ > jidaḥ*, 'glass'; *gh > q* is infrequent, *ghashmar > qashmar*, 'to fool', Tur, *qashmér*, 'to fool'.

t > th, tūt > tūth, 'berries'; *t > d, 'akrūt > 'akrūd*, 'steam' (Eng) > *ṣdīm*. *t > ṭ* , *tos*, Tur, > *ṭos*, 'dust'; *ṣit > siṭ*, 'fame', 'repute'.

h > kh, hudlī-l-çāy! > khudrī -l-çāy, 'brew the tea!'

h > ḥ, qiḥar for *qihar*, 'to be upset', and *ḥ> h, farḥāt > farhād*, a woman's name.

ṭ > d, qaṭīfah > qadīfah; *faqaṭ*, 'only' > *faqad*.

j > ç, wajih > waçih, 'face; *ajlaḥ > açlaḥ*, 'without hair on the face'.

dh > ḍ, dhāq/g > ḍāq/g, 'he tasted'; *dhirā' > ḍra'*, 'arm'.

hamza > ', antīkah > 'antīkah, 'antique'; *armūd* for *'armūt*, 'pears'.

l > n, silsilah > sinsilah, 'chain'; *mi'çān > mi'çāl*, 'a sling shot'.

n > l, arman > armal, 'Armenians'; *khamman > khammal*, 'to think'.

r > l, za'bal for *za'bar*, 'to cheat', *mfarṭaḥ > mfalṭaḥ*, 'flatten'.

s > z, almāz for *almās*, 'diamond'; *handazah* for *handasah*, 'geometry'.

d > t , *sādis > sātis*, *Farhād > Farḥāt*, a woman's name; *d > ṭ*, *lokandah* for *loqanṭah*, a type of perfume; *armūd > 'armūt*, 'pears'.

Marjal; 'to make s.o. behave like a man', *tmarjal*, 'to claim to be like a man', (*Mu'jam*, 111) < *rajul*, 'man'.

Marshag, 'to throw' (stones), < *rashaqa*, CA, 'same', (Sām, 181), *marshag lah*, 'he said that someone has many bad attributes' < *mirshāg*, which is an epithet for a penis (Ḥana, *Mu'jam*, III, 188; Kāmil, 15), but *mirshagh* means, 'a piece of wood that the weavers use'.

Mashghal, *tmashghal*, 'to do light work or pretend to work', *shugul*, IA, 'work'.

Mashkal, 'to complicate a situation'; 'to cause problems', (Wood, 439) < *mushkilah*, 'a problem'.

Maskhar, *tmaskhar*, 'to ridicule', (Ḥana, *Mu'jam*, II, 111) < *sakhira*, 'to mock'; (Bak, 132; DH, *Qāmūs*, 66), or < *maskharah*, 'an object of ridicule'.

Maṣqal and *masqal*, 'to polish', 'to beautify', 'to flatter', 'to be a hypocrite', Arm, *masqōléh*, (YM I, *Hebrew-Aramaic*, 275; Soko, 829). Some say *qaṣmal*, 'to beautify' (metathesis), *mgaṣmal*, (*q* > *g*), 'neat', 'beautiful', (Qad, II: 277[50]).

Mazgagh, *tmazgagh*, 'to provoke by bumping s.o.' (Bak, 132).

Mazlaq/g, (tr.), 'to make s.o. slip', (Wood, 438) < *zalaqa*, 'to slip', CA, *tmazlaq/g*, 'to slip a lot', (Ḥana, *Mu'jam*, II, 111).

B. 1.6. Type, T, Ṭ. 2.3.4

The *t* as a prefixed morpheme has been widely utilized in the formation of nominal patterns in Arabic. Arabic nouns with prefixed *t* may express a variety of concepts and ideas like abstract nouns and verbal nouns. Quadriliteral verbs which begin with the consonant *t* as a prefix to triliteral verbs in IA are very few; however, such types of verbs exist in Egyptian Arabic and Amharic (Kāmil, 15).

In the formation of quadriliteral verbs, the *t* element may be prefixed to triradical nouns, verbs and stems, thus, it retains its position as the initial radical. In some cases the source noun cannot be traced to a specific verb or stem, but seems to have several possible stems or it is borrowed. The initial *t* throughout the conjugation is often assimilated to the first radical of the triliteral verb when that radical is a sun letter except, *t*, *r*, *l* and *n*, as in *iddahdar*, for *itdahdar*, 'to roll down', (Mac, II, 427).

Talfas, 'to squander', (Ḥana, *Mu'jam*, II, 104) < *fils*, an Iraqi currency of a very little value.

---

50 Ḥusayn Qaddūrī, *Lu'ab wa-Aghānī al-Aṭfāl al-Sha'biyyah fī al-'Irāq* (Baghdad 1975), (henceforth Qad).

Tandal, 'to let down', 'to lower' < *dandal*, 'same', (Cha, *Ath*, 44; Ḥajj, *al-Amthāl*, 46).

Ṭangar, ('Awwād, 24), 'to be angry', (Ḥana, *al-Alfāẓ*, 239). In the United Arab Emirates (UAE), 'same', (Ḥanẓal, 426[51]).

Tanḥar, ('Awwād, 23), 'to be angry', (Sām, 155) < *ḥiran*, (metathesis), 'to be angry and stubborn', (Ḥana, *Mu'jam*, II, 121).

Tanfakh, 'to swell because of anger', 'to inflate', (DH, *Qāmūs*, 181), *nafakha*, CA, 'same'.

Ṭarkhan and *tarshan*, 'to have a hoarse voice', (Ḥana, *Mu'jam*, II, 53 and 55); 'to become sour' < Per, *tarkhīnah*, a type of food which tastes sour, (Bak, 320, Cha, *Kalimāt*, 136).

Tartakh, 'to become soft' (bread in soup), (Ḥana, *Mu'jam*, II, 52). It is likely that *takhtakh* > *tartakh*, or it is a compound of *tar*, Per, 'wet', and CA, *takhkha*, 'to become soggy'.

Tashqal, 'to cheat' < *tishqaltā*, Arm, *shqal*, 'to swindle', (Bak, 121; Ḥana, *Mu'jam*, II, 680); 'to estimate' (weight), (Wood, 57; Cha, *Ath*, 25), Arm, *metashqōléh*, (YM I, *Hebrew-Aramaic*, 312).

Taslagh, 'to skin' < *taslakh*, *silakh*; *taslāq* 'hairless', 'naked', (Gīl, 248), OTur, *tāslāq*.

Ṭazban, ('Awwād, 24) , Syr, *zbān*, 'to bargain', 'to buy', (YM I, *Hebrew-Aramaic*, 379).

B. 1.7. Type B, or D, Ḥ, L, 2.3.4

The following are triliteral verbs in IA prefixed with one of the above radicals:

Baḥlaq/g, 'to stare', 'to open one's eyes wide', (Mac, 421; Sām, 152; DH, *Qāmūs*, 36), √ BLQ.

Ḥamlaqa, CA, 'same', *m* > *b*, then the *b* exchanged position with *h* > *baḥlaq/g*, (metathesis). One has to consider also that *baḥlaq* is a result of dissimilation of *ballaqa*, *-ll-* > *-ḥl-*, 'to stare', (Ḥana, *Mu'jam*, I, 468), *baḥlaq* 'to open the eyes wide', (Bak, 73; Mac, I, 433).

Da'bal, 'to hurl down', YD, 209; 'to roll' (tr.), (Ḥana, *Mu'jam*, III, 59), 'to make a round shape', (Mac, I, 416), 'to roll into a ball', (Wood, 158; Sām, 161; AF,

51 Al-Fāliḥ Ḥanẓal, *al-Alfāẓ al-'Āmmiyyah fī Dawlat al-Imārāt al-'Arabiyyah al-Muttaḥidah* (Abu Dhabi 1998), (henceforth Ḥanẓal).

Mu'jam, 54) < *'abula* (al-Karmilī, *Majmū'ah*, II, 184, n. 49) < *dahbala*, CA, 'same', or < *dabala* (Sam 161; Bak, 219).

Daghmash, 'to become blurry' (sight), *ghamisha*, or < *taghmash*, 'same', (Ḥana, *Mu'jam*, III, 63).

Dahlaz, 'to flatter', (Gīl, 93; YD, *Sefat*, 207).

Daghmar, 'to hide s.th.', (Ḥana, *Mu'jam*, III, 62), *ghamara*, 'to soak'.

Dahwar, ('Awwād, 23), 'to roll down' < *hāra*, CA, 'to collapse', √ HWR; *itdahwar*, 'to get worse' (health), (Ḥana, *Mu'jam*, III, 116).

Danfash, and *damfash*, 'to flap up or out' (feathers, hair), 'to have unkempt hair', (Thin, 151); *n* > *m*, 'to become arrogant', (Gīl, 92; YD, *Sefat*, 112; Sām, 162), 'to blow a lot' (intr.) < Per, *dah*, 'ten' and *nafasha*, CA (Ḥana, *Mu'jam*, III, 89).

La'waj, √ 'WJ 'to bend' (metals), (Thin, 191), *la'waj ilqaḍiyyah*, 'he complicated the matter'.

Lahmad ('Awwād, 25), 'to fade away', 'to abate' < *hamada*, CA, 'same'.

Lakbash, 'to hang s.th. up with a nail', (Bak, 445), see also *kalbaç*.

B. 2. Quadriradical Verbs Resulting from Triradical Verbs Augmented by an Infix after the First Radical of the Triliteral Verb

B. 2.1. Type 1. R. 3.4[52]

There are instances showing that infixes in Semitic languages are a result of dissimilation and that there is considerable freedom to produce these dissimilated forms in some Arabic dialects and in neo-Syriac (O'Leary, 216). The most frequent infixes in Semitic languages are *r*, *l*, *n* and rarely *m*, *b*, *h*, *ḥ*, ʿ and *ṭ* (Moscati, 130–1; Kāmil, 9). In many of the following quadriradical verbs in IA, for example, the augmented verbs through the infix *r* indicate intensification or frequency of action and are generated by dissimilation of the triradical verbs (Form II). However, several of these verbs, are borrowed. Examples:

Barsaq, (*'Awwād*, 22), 'to become long' (branch) < *basaqa*, 'to stare', (*Muḥīṭ*, 40).

Barṭa', 'to gallop' (horse), (DH, *Qāmūs*, 39), 'to open the legs apart', (Bak, 359), 'to jump' (horse) √ *B'Ṭ*, Heb, *ba'aṭ*, 'to kick'.

'Arqal, 'to hinder'; 'to complicate', (Wood, 308) < *'aqala*, 'to tie'.

Bar'aṭ and *bal'aṭ*, (*r* > *l*) 'to flop' (fish) < *lubaṭ* , 'to wiggle', as in *has-simaç tāzah u-ba'dah yilbuṭ*, 'the fish are fresh and still wiggling', (Wood, 417) < Syr, (FM, 64); 'to roll in dust', (Ḥana, *Mu'jam*, I, 589) , *tbal'aṭ*, 'to roll on the ground due to poisoning or stomach ache', (Ḥana, *Mu'jam*, II, 25). This verb, in general, denotes unbalanced movement.

Darbak, 'to bang strongly' (door, drum) and 'to make a lot of noise', dissim. of *dabbaka* *-bb-* > *rb-* (Sām, 160), < CA, *darabūkka*, a one-headed hand drum.

Darfa', 'to shove', 'to push to the ground' < *daffa'a* (Wood, 156), dissim. *-ff-* > *-rf-* (Sām, 161); 'to expel', (Gīl, 90); 'to get rid of', or < *dafa'a*, 'to push', (Ḥana, *al-Alfāẓ*, 131). The *r* is an infix.

Furqa' or *furga'*, 'to heat to a boiling point that makes noise' (oil), (Wood, 351) *faqa'a*, 'to bubble', 'to burst', (Sām, 173; Thin, 111; Ḥana, *al-Alfāẓ*, 173), 'to disperse', (cloud).

Farṭaḥ, *barṭaḥ*, 'to widen, flatten' < CA, 'same', or dissim. *faṭṭaḥa*, 'same', *ṭṭ* > *rṭ* (Sām, 174).

Falṭaḥ, (ʿAwwād, 24), see *farṭaḥ*, (*r* > *l*).

---

52 For examples of quadriliteral verbs with infixes in other Arabic dialects, see Ṭobī, 72–5, 77, Kāmil, 12–13 (in the Arabic part, and pp. 9–40 in the non-Arabic part).

Gardash, 'to gnaw', 'to cut s.th. with the teeth', (Cha, *Ath*, 74; Baz, 153; Soko, 302; Thin, 160).

Sardaḥ, ('Awwād, 23 < *shardaḥa* < *radaḥa*).

Karbal, 'to press and make s.th ball-shaped', (Bak, 413).

Kardash, *gardash* and *kaghdash* ('Ubaydī, 54; Ghanīmah, 268[53]; Bak, 414) < *kadasha*, or *kaddasha*, CA, 'same', (Sām, 179), dissim. *-dd-*> *-rd-*; Arm, *kardash*, (Cha, *Ath*, 74; Soko, 302).

Karmash, CA, 'same', Arm, *kmash*, 'to contract' (muscle), (DH, *Qāmūs*, 235), 'to become wrinkled', (Wood, 403); 'to wither', (Mélaméd, 479) < *kamasha*, CA, 'to shrink because of cold or heat', (Sām, 179), *mkarmash*, 'spotted', as in the saying *wuççah mkarmash çanna gishir raggī*, 'his face is freckled like a watermelon's peel', (Ḥajj I, 118[54], Ḥajj II, 488[55]).

Ḥarmaḍ, 'to become sour'< *ḥammaḍ*, 'same', dissim. *-mm-* > *-rm-*.

Jarba', *jaghba'*, 'to become wrinkled, weak', 'to shrink', (Gīl, 53; YD, *Sefat*, 139) < *jaba'a*, CA, 'to be weak'.

Jardam/jaghdham/jardham, 'to be infected with leprosy or any skin blemish', (Ḥana, *Mu'jam*, II, 200) < *jarrada*, 'to peel', 'to make an uneven surface', (Bak, 144), 'to crush', Arm, *gardam*, 'to cut into pieces', (Cha, *Ath*, 30; Sām, 155). The *r* here is an infix resulting from the dissimilation of *jadhdhama*, *-dhdh-* > *-rdh* (Kāmil, 56; Bak, 142).

Kharbat, 'to toss or drop s.o. to the ground', (Sām, 177), *kabaḥa*, 'same' in CA, hence, the *r* in *karbaḥ* is an infix, However, this infix is due to the dissimilation of *bb* > *rb-* in *kabbaḥa*.

Karbal, 'to roll s.th. into a round and accurate shape', (MM, 306; Sām, 178), 'to overburden, overload', (Wood, 401).

Karbas, *kaghbas* < *kabbasa*, CA, 'to push to the ground', dissim. *-bb-* > *-rb-* (Sām, 178; Bak, 414; 'Ubaydī, 50) < *kibas*, IA, 'to press', 'to put s.o. in an inescapable situation', (Wood, 401, fig.), *tkarbas*, 'to fall to the ground', (Bak, 130). It is attested in the Kuwaitī dialect with the same meaning (Ḥana, *al-Alfaẓ*, 295).

Kardaḥ, ('Awwād, 24), more common is *takardaḥ*, 'to be shrunk', CA, *kadaḥa*, CA, 'same'.

---

53 Y. Ghanīmah, 'al-Alfāẓ al-'Ārāmiyyah fī al-Lughah al-'Irāqiyyah', *Lisān al-'Arab*, IV (December, 1926), 265–71, (henceforth Ghanīmah).

54 'Azīz al-Ḥajjiyyah, *Baghdādiyyāt* I (Baghdad 1967), (henceforth Ḥajj I).

55 'Azīz al-Ḥajjiyyah, *Baghdādiyyāt* II (Baghdad 1968), (henceforth Ḥajj II).

Karfat, 'to shove', (Wood, 402; Cha, *Kalimāt*, 163; AF, *Mu'jam*, 151) < *kifat*, 'to throw from a high place', (Bak, 414) < *guruftan*, Per, 'to catch and imprison', (Bak, 130), *tkarfat*, 'to be shoved', (Ḥana, *Mu'jam*, II, 93).

Karsaḥ, 'to expel', 'to drive away'< *kassḥ*, dissim. *-ss-* > *-rs-*, 'same', (Bak, 409) or < 'to become *kasīḥ*, CA, 'paralyzed', (DH, *Qāmūs*, 272).

Kharbaq , and *ḥarbaq*, Syr, *ḥbaq*, 'to intertwine', 'to clasp' < *ḥabbaqa*, 'to hug', 'to complicate', (DH, *Qāmūs*, 87; Ghanīmah, 270); Arm, *mékharbōqéh*, (YM I, *Hebrew-Aramaic*, 259), 'same'; 'to throw into disorder', (Wood, 131; Ben-Jacob, *Hebrew and Aramaic*, 166); 'to spoil a setting', (Mac, I, 421; Gīl, 76); 'to talk nonsense', (Ḥana, *Mu'jam*, II, 476; Shāl, I, 490[56]), *tkharbaq*, 'to fall and hurt one's leg', (YD, *Sefat*, 173).

Kharbaṣ, 'to intertwine' (thread), 'to mess up'; 'to put in disorder' < *khabbaṣa*, 'same', dissim. *-bb-* > *-rb-* (Sām, 159) or < *khabaṣa* (Ḥana, *Mu'jam*, II, 475; Thin, 159).

Kharbaṭ, 'to mix up', (Erwin, *A Short Reference*, 79; Ben-Jacob, *Hebrew and Aramaic*, 166); 'to mess up', as in *agūm 'aléh wakharbiṭ gharāḍ wijha*, 'I'll get up and mess up his face', (Ḥana, *Mu'jam*, II, 476), or *khabbaṭa* > *kharbaṭa*, a dissim. of *-bb-* > *-rb-* (Sām, 159; Bak, 189) or < *khubaṭ*, 'to mix', (Wood, 128) , *tkharbaṭ*, 'to be in disorder, confusion', 'to get worse' (health), as in *lamma-l-marīḍ fakkata-l-ṣkhūnah, akal timman wu-tkharbaṭ*, 'When the fever was gone' (lit. 'let go of him'), 'the sick man ate rice and got worse', 'to become sick and near death', (Mac, I, 432); Arm, *mékharboṭéh*, (YM II, *Aramaic-Kurdish*, 259), 'to intertwine' (strings). It is possible that *kharbaṭ* is a *naḥt* of *khalaṭa+khabaṭa*.

Kharmash, *kharbash*, (tr. and intr.), 'to scratch', (Erwin, *A Short Reference*, 78; Gīl, 77; DH, *Qāmūs*, 98; Shāl, II, 203). It also could be the result of dissimilation of *khammasha* (Sām, 159), *'mm-* > *-rm-* then *rm* > *rb*, Arm, *mékharbōshé*, (YM II, *Aramaic-Kurdish*, 259; 'Ubaydī, 71), √ KhDSh or √ KhRM.

Ra'bal, 'to tear' (dress), CA, 'same'; 'to muddle', (Ḥana, *Mu'jam*, III, 192), *mra'bal*, 'untidy person', (Sam, 163).

Marwaj, more commonly *tmarwaj*, 'to move and shake', dissim. *mawwaj*, *-ww-* > *rw*, 'to make waves', (Thin, 211; Sām, 181).

Nafrash, (*'alā*), 'to speak to s.o. with firmness and arrogance', (Thin, 248), *tnafrash*, 'to become ruthless, haughty', (Ḥana, *Mu'jam*, II, 123; MM, 300), < *nafasha*, 'to flap up or out' (feathers, hair).

56 'Abbūd al-Shāljī, *Mawsū'at al-Kināyāt al-'Āmmiyyah al-Baghdādiyyah* I (Beirut 1979), (henceforth Shāl, I).

Qaghḍam, (Mosul),[57] *garḍam* (Baghdad) 'to gnaw', (Gīl, 217), as one may do with her/his nails when confused < *qaḍama*, CA, 'same', (Cha, *Ath*, 33), 'to punch', (Wood, 387), *tqaghḍam*, 'to be without patience', (Bak, 129), 'to be annoyed and bored' (fig.), (Ḥana, *Mu'jam*, II, 98).

Qarfaṣ, 'to squat on the ground' (with thighs against the stomach and arms enfolding the legs) < *qaffaṣa*, 'same', (Sām, 176; DH, *Qāmūs*, 222; Wehr, 759)< *qafaṣa* (*Muḥīṭ*, 750), 'same'.

Qarma', *garma'*, 'to hit the fingers of the hand' < *qama'a*, CA, 'to strike the fingers with a piece of wood or iron', (Thin, 164; Sām, 176).

Garmadh, 'to contract o.s. due to cold', (Thin, 164) <*jarmaz*, CA, 'same'.

Gharmadh, 'to be stingy' < *qarmaṭ*, 'to be thrifty', (Thin, 164).

Qarṭam, *garṭam*, 'to cut off' < *qaṭama*, 'to, cut, nibble'; Syr, 'to cut branches off trees', 'to shorten', (Sām, 175; DH, *Qāmūs*, 222); Arm, *qéraṭa*, 'to nibble', (YM II, *Aramaic-Kurdish*, 401).

Ṣarga', *ṣarqa'* < *ṣaqa'a*, 'to strike', (Sām, 169; Ḥana, *Mu'jam*, II, 70), more commonly *tṣarga'*, 'to be afraid' (as if by thunder) < *taṣaqqa'a*, 'he was frightened by thunder', dissim. *-qq-* > *-rq-* (Ḥana, *al-Alfāẓ*, 216), or < *ṣiga'*, IA, 'to slap on top of the head', (Wood, 267).

---

57 A few characteristics of the Arabic dialect of Mosul are:
People there pronounce *r* as g, like the Christian and the Jews in Baghdad. However *r* is maintained in a few words (See al-Mallāh, 'Nukāt', 349–53; al-Sāmarrā'ī, 1968, and al-Dabbāgh,1956, I: 8–16).

a. *s* > *ṣ*, as in, *sath* > *ṣath*; *ḥasrah* > *ḥaṣrah*, 'sigh', *saqī'*, 'frost', for *ṣaqī'*, *jaraṣ*, 'bell' for *jaras*. The change of *ṣ* to *s* is less common.

b. ç < *k*, *çidhib* for *kithib* > 'a lie'.

c. *z* > *th* , *dayyūz* for *dayyūth*.

d. *t* > *ṭ*, *ṭghāb*, 'dust' for *turāb*, *tirrahāṭ* for *tirrahāt*, 'nonsense'.

e. ' for ', *'āhirah* for *'āhirah*, 'whore'.

f. Another feature of the Mosul dialect is *imālah*, i.e. the pronunciation of a shaded *e*.

g. There are a few sounds which change to other sounds in some words, but maintain their sounds in others, e.g. *d/dh*, *q/g*, as in *qasha'* and *gasha'*, 'to see'; *qāl* and *gāl* 'he said'; *b/m*, as in *mismār* and *bismār*, 'a nail'; *ṣ*, *s* and *z*, as in *lasaq/lazaq/laṣaq*, 'to glue'.

h. Christian and Jews in Baghdad and Mosul pronounce *r* as *gh*, however *r* is maintained in a few words among them attributes of God as in 'Abd al-Raḥmān, 'Abd al-Razzāq, etc.

i. *r* > *gh* is common in Mosul, as in *ḥajar*, 'stones' > *ḥajagh*, *ghūḥ*! for *rūḥ*!, 'go!'. Such a change is not used in mentioning God's attributes and other words like *yishkir*, 'he thanks' and *yidhker*, 'he remembers'. *ḥ*. *dh* > (ḍ), like *ydhūq* > *yḍūq*, 'he tastes'.

The suffix *hā'* 'his', 'its' (m.) is replaced by *u*, *kitābahu* > *ktābu*, 'his book'. In the I and VIII verb Forms, a *hamzah* is added to the 3ms and 3fs imperfect as in *'iyghīd*, 'he wants', *ittafaq*, 'he agreed'. The ending *t* of singular nouns and adjectives changes to a long *yā'*, e.g. *Fāṭmah*, *ṭwīlah*, 'tall' > *Faṭmī* and *ṭwīlī*, but in a few words no such change occurs, as in *qṣīghah*, 'short', *ḥijghah*, 'small room'.

Sharbak, 'to interlock', 'to entangle', 'to tie firmly' < *shabbaka*, dissim. *-bb-* >- *rb-* (Wood, 240) < Syr, *sharbūgha*, (MM, 276), (see also below, C. 3.2) .

Warsha', 'to surround, s.o.' < *washsha'a*, CA, dissim. *-shsh-* >*rsh-*, more commonly *tawarsha'a*, 'to assail s.o.' (vulg.), *twarsha' il-mawjūd*, 'he ate everything', (Thin, 266, n. 25; Ḥana, *Mu'jam*, II, 133).

Sharmakh, 'to scratch', (Shāl, II, 620) < *kharmash*, 'same'; 'to become worn out cloth' like an old sword, *rmāh*, Syr, 'same'. The *shīn* is a prefix.

Qarnaṣ, *garnas*, 'to make a zigzag edge', 'to prick somebody's skin', 'to scallop', 'to crouch' (Wood, 372, Sām, 181), Syr, *qras*, 'to freeze because of cold', (AF, *Mu'jam*, 139; Sām, 177); 'to fly high' in the language of birdwatchers (Shāl, II, 380).

Zarnaq, 'to drink water from a bowl without having the lips touching it', 'to fall (water) from a high place making a sound', (Thin, 73; Ḥana, *Mu'jam*, III, 288; DH, *Qāmūs*, 130), dissim. of *zannaqa*, *-nn-* > *-rn-*, or Arm, *zarnūqah*, 'a spring whose water falls from a high place', (AF, *Mu'jam*, 71), or *zaraqa*, 'to drip'. The *n* is an infix.

Zarwat, 'to eat in a hurry', 'to swallow food quickly without chewing it'; (Bak, 239).

Zarwaq, ('Awwād, 23), 'to dilute with water', (Bak, 239; Wood, 203); 'to decorate', 'to adorn' < *zawwaqa*, 'to beautify', dissim. *-ww-* > *-rw-*.

B. 2.2. Type 1. N. 3.4

Examples:

'Ajraf, *t'ajraf*, 'to be arrogant', (Wood, 302).

'Anfaṣ, 'to kick angrily' (donkey), 'to be stubborn', ('Ubaydī, 50; Gīl, 176; Thin, 96), 'to jump and kick' (donkey), 'to make sounds like a horse or a donkey', (Bak, 345), *'affaṣa*, 'to kick a lot' and the *n* is a result of dissimilation (YD, *Sefat*, 273), 'to break the rope and be free' < *'afaṣa*, 'to uproot the pole of a tent', (Sām, 172; Thin, 96). It also is used as an epithet for a person who opposes others and is stubborn, (Shāl, II, 418).

'Anjar, 'to beat up', 'to strike on the head and cause a lump', dissim. of *'ajjara*, *jj* > *nj*, (Sām, 172; Wood, 325), *ta'anjar 'anjarah zénah*, 'he really got his lumps', *'anjūrah*, 'swelling', 'lump', *m'anjir*, 'person who is hard to get along with', 'a rude person', (Wood, 325). In CA, *'ajjarah* means 'to stretch and fold the lips' < dissim. *-jj-* > *-nj-*, 'to smack the lips'.

'Ankash < *'akana* or a composition of *'akana* and *'akasha*, 'to frown', (Sām, 172; Bak, 346; Thin, 92); 'to be dry', 'to shrink out of fear or cold', (Gīl, 172; YD, *Sefat*, 234; Ḥana, *al-Alfāẓ*, 269), *'akasha*, 'to appear in clusters' (fruits).

'Anjar, 'to beat s.o. black and blue', *t'anjar*; 'to become swollen from beating', (Wood, 325).

'Anqad, 'to grow blossoms'; 'to complicate' < *'aqqada*, dissim. *-qq-* > *-nq'*, (YD, *Sefat*, 208).

'Antak, 'to show off', 'to act out', (Wood, 325).

T'antak 'alā, 'to treat s.o. rudely', (Thin, 96); 'to become quarrelsome', (Mac, I, 436).

'Antal, 'to tear into pieces', (MM, 225).

'Antar, 'to become erect' (penis); *t'antar*, 'to be distended', (Wood, 325) < *'attara*, CA (Thin, 96) , dissim. *-tt-* > *-nt*, *'antar 'idhānah*, 'to prick up one's ears', (Ḥana, *al-Alfāẓ*, 195).

Fanghar, 'to open widely', 'to gape' (a wound), Heb. *pa'ar*, 'same'. The *n* is an infix (Sām, 175).

Shantar, (tr., intr.), 'to prick up the ear', 'to make s.th. stand', (MM, 211; Bak, 302; Cha, *Ath*, 90; Ḥana, *al-Alfāẓ*, 195; Baz, 110); *tashantar*, 'to behave in a vulgar manner', 'to act up', (Wood, 250; Sām, 168).

Dangar, 'to duck, lower' (the head), *dannaka*, CA (Bak, 226), < *dannag*, or *dannaç*, *dannaj* ('Awwād, 23), 'to bend', (Ḥana, *Mu'jam*, III, 87), dissim. *-nn-* > *-ng-*; (Wood, 166), as an Iraqi folk poet said, *shifithā timshī bil-sūsah béḍ il-ḥamām dyūsah dangarit tabūsah [dabūsah], dangar wayyāya ḥṣanī*, (al-'Ānī, 199[58]), 'I saw her walking in the village, her breasts [like] eggs of doves. I bent to kiss her, my horse hunkered down after me'.

Dangaz, 'to lower the head', (Ḥana, *Mu'jam*, III, 91), CA , 'same', more common in use are the verbs *dannaç* and *dannag*.

Fanghar, 'to open' (wound) 'to flow' (blood) < *faghghara*, 'to open' (mouth) (Sām, 175), dissim. *-ghgh-* > *-ngh-*.

Fanjakh, 'to open the legs wide when sitting or standing' < *fashaja*, CA, 'same', (Thin, 118, n. 64).

Fanjal, 'to make big' < *fajjala*, CA, dissim. *-jj-* > *-nj-*, *tfanjal* , 'to enjoy o.s.' (Bak, 128). The following saying, *yā zar' lā-titfanjal ghada yijīk il-manjal*, 'O plant, don't

58 Walīd al-'Anī, 'Aghānī Sha'biyyah min 'Ānah', *al-Turāth al-Sha'bī* V, (Baghdad 1975), 199–204, (henceforth al-'Ānī).

rejoice, tomorrow the scythe will cut you' (lit. 'will come to you'), (Cha, *Kalimāt*, 41), is said to be a warning that there is no escape from death.

Fanjar, 'to stare', 'to glare' (DH, *Qāmūs*, 214), as in *fanjar 'énah'*. This verb is attested in the Lebanese dialect (AF, *Mu'jam*, 133; Wehr, 729).

Ḥanbaq, 'to be spoiled, fermented', (Bak, 199) < *ḥabaqa*, CA, 'same'.

Ḥanbaṭ, 'to become swollen in the face out of anger', (Sām, 158), dissim of *ḥabbaṭa*, where *-bb-* >- *nb-*.

Ḥandal, 'to carry on the shoulder' < *ḥaddala* , dissim. *-dd-* > *-nd-* (Sām, 158) , more commonly *tḥandal*, 'to hang on a rope or a piece of wood and dangle', (Bak, 115; Ḥana, *Mu'jam*, II, 38, 419; Mac, I, 421; Gīl, 147).

Hanjal, 'to jump up and down on one foot', 'to hop, bounce', (Sām, 183; Wood, 483); 'to run slowly' < *hajjala*, 'same', dissim. *–jj-> -nj-*.

Ḥantaf, 'to desire', 'to covet', (DH, *Qāmūs*, 90), or a composition of *ḥaffa*, 'to depilate' + *natafa*, 'to pluck', 'to be stingy'; Syr, *ḥtaf*, or < *ḥattafa*, 'to carve', 'to cut' (meat), dissim. *-tt-* > *-nt-* √ ḤTF.

Hantar, 'to speak firmly' < *hatr*, 'a lie', (Thin, 287).

Jandal, 'to knock down flat to the ground', (Mac, I, 416) < *jaddala* (Ḥana, *Mu'jam*, II, 240), 'same', dissim. *-dd* > *-nd*, 'to tighten strongly', (Sām, 156)

Janzar, < *zanjar* (metathesis), 'to become rusty', (DH, *Qāmūs*, 80; Bak, 252), Arm, *zingārā*, Per, *zinjār*, 'rust', (Shīr, 80[59]; TA, 33[60]; MM, 179, Bak; 252; Ḥana, *Mu'jam*, III, 263; Sām, 188; Cha, *Kalimāt*, 105).

Kan'as, 'to be bad' (fruits) < Arm, *k'īsa*, 'same', (Cha, *Ath*, 84).

Kanrash, 'to shrink' < *karīsha* , CA, 'same'.

Khanbaq, 'to be fermented and spoiled' (milk) (Bak, 199; 'Ubaydī, 52).

Khançar, var. of *kanzar*. In CA, 'to become fat like a pig' (*khanzīr*).

Khandal, 'to change one's mind' < *khaddala*, CA, 'same', dissim. *-dd-* > *-nd-*; *tkhandal*, 'to become confused and hesitant'.

Khanfar, 'to open one's nostrils as a result of fear, anger, or excitement', (FM, 497; Sām, 159), < *khaffara*, CA, dissim. *-ff-* > *-nf-*, 'to snuggle', (Sām, 160).

Khanjal, 'to be ashamed, embarrassed' < *khajila*, 'same', (Ḥana, *Mu'jam*, II, 535).

Khanṭal, 'to stare angrily', (Wood, 147; Naqqāsh, *Nzūlah*, 205), 'to lower the head'; (Ḥana, *Mu'jam*, II, 535); 'to sit with a grave expression because of a calamity'

---

59 Addī Shīr, *Mu'jam al-Alfāẓ al-Fārisiyyah al-Mu'arrabah* (Beirut 1980), (henceforth Shīr).

60 Ṭūbyā al-'Unaysī, *Kitāb al-Alfāẓ al-Dakhīlah fī al-Lughah al-'Arabiyyah* (Egypt 1932), (henceforth TA).

(Mosul), (Bak, 200); 'to put to shame' < *khaṭṭala* CA, dissim. *ṭṭ* > *nṭ*, 'to be depressed', (Sām, 159), *mkhanṭal*, 'a slow and lazy person', (Wood, 245).

Khanzar, 'to look at maliciously', 'to stare angrily', (Wood, 147; Ḥana, *Mu'jam*, II, 533–4), dissim. of *khazzara*, *-zz-* > *-nz* (the *n* is a suffix) (Sām, 159); 'to have a gloomy face', (MM, 302); 'to lose speech because of sickness', (Bak, 199).

Qan'ar and *qanbar*, 'to speak from the base of the throat', (Shāl, II, 323), 'to show off', 'to give o.s. airs', (Wood, 380; Ḥana, *Mu'jam*, II, 90) < *qa''ara*, CA, and the *n* is a result of dissim. *-''-* > *-n'-*, 'to sit for a short time with one leg raised', (Thin, 178); 'to fill to the top of the glass', (Bak, 395); 'to misbehave', (Sām, 177).

Qanbaṣ and *gambaṣ*, 'to hunker down', (Wood, 394); 'to sit on feet raised without touching the ground', (Bak, 434; Thin, 178) < *qamaṣa*, 'same', (*b* > m), CA (Sām, 177).

Qanza', 'to prick', 'to flee from a rooster fighting another rooster', (Thin, 178; *Muḥīṭ*, 758) < *kanza'a*, CA, 'to have a front seat', 'preside over', Syr, *kunzī'ah*, 'a strong branch of a tree', (FM, 497) or < *qanzū'ah*; 'the crest of a rooster', 'a strip of hair in the middle of a shaved head', (Bak, 397); 'to stand alone', (Sām, 190); 'to pull a fast one', 'to trick', (Wood, 379).

Ṣanba', *ṣamba'*, 'to sit uninvited in the middle of a group' (Christians in Mosul) < (Bak, 310). In CA, 'to get up, stand up', or 'to point with a finger' (*iṣba'*) < ṣabbaʿa, CA.

Ṣanbar, 'to claim', (Sām, 169), 'to show', dissim. *ṣabbara*, *-bb-> -nb*.

Ṣandaḥ, 'to make bald', (Sām, 169) < *ṣaddaḥa*, 'to be bald', CA, dissim. *-dd-* > *-nd-*.

Sankar, 'to be enraged' < *sankīrah*, 'rage', (Ḥajj, *al-Amthāl*, 119[61]; al-Karmilī, *Majmū'ah*, II, 277, n. 41; Shāl, II, 173; Sām, 166; Bak, 254). It may be a distortion of *zangar*, 'to be angry', or *sakkara* where *kk* > *nk*. In CA, 'to act in a state of drunkenness' < *sankīrah*, 'a state of losing one's common sense and becoming angry'.

Shanbaṭ, 'to swell in anger', (Sām, 167), 'to jump' (fish) < dissim. *shabbaṭa -bb-> -nb*.

Shandal, 'to flatter s.o. in order to cause trouble' < *shaddala*, CA, 'same', Syr, *shdal*, (FM, 30–6; AF, *Mu'jam*, 100), Heb, *shiddēl*, 'to persuade', 'to incite'.

Shankhar, 'to snore loudly', ShKhR or NKhR (AF, *Mu'jam*, 100) < *shakhara*.

Shanṭagh, 'to cheat', (YD, *Sefat*, 152).

61 'Azīz al-Ḥajjiyyah, *al-Amthāl wal-Kināyāt fī Shi'r al-Mullah 'Abbūd al-Karkhī* (Baghdad 1986), (henceforth Ḥajj, *al-Amthāl*)

Ṭanbar and *ṭambar*, 'to be angry', 'to swell in anger', (Shāl, II, 312; Ḥana, *al-Alfāẓ*, 353), dissim. of *ṭabbara*, *bb* > *nb-* , or < *ṭanaba*, 'to rise' (belly); 'to be rude', (Sām, 170; DH, *Qāmūs*, 181), 'to show dissatisfaction or anger', (MM, 222).

Zan'ar, 'to bray a lot, like a donkey', (Bak, 253; Ḥana, *Mu'jam*, III, 264; Sām, 155, 146), Syr, *n'ar* (FM, 226), or *za''ara*, 'to be very angry', dissim. -*''*- > -*n'*-.

Zangar, 'to be angry', (Bak, 254; Cha, *Kalimāt*, 105). See also *sankar*.

B. 2.3. Type 1. W. 3.4

Several verbs of the type *faw'al*, *fō'al* and *fé'al* are, in fact, one Form. They are alternatives to verb Forms I, II, III and V or are loan verbs or derived from nouns. Examples:

'Ō'ā, var. of *'aw'aw*, 'to bark', 'to scream', (Turj, 88), 'to crow'; (Erwin, *A Short Reference*, 79; Bak, 220; Mac, II, 415), Syr, '*Ō'ā yā*, Akk, *'āw'ī*, 'sound of a baby crying', (FM, 399; Cha, *Ath*, 67).

'Ōkar and *'awkar*, 'to make turbid' (water), (Bak, 269; DH, *Qāmūs*, 198), *'akira*, CA, 'to become turbid'.

'Ōmad, 'to stand up', 'to support s.th with a pillar' (*'amūd*), *t'ōmad*, 'to be stiff', Heb, *'amad*, 'to stand', (Ben-Jacob, *Hebrew and Aramaic*, 119; Avīshūr, 226).

'Ōnash, 'to punish', Heb, *'anash* (Ben-Jacob, *Hebrew and Aramaic*, 22), *t'ōnash'*, 'to be punished', (Ben-Jacob, *Hebrew and Aramaic*, 153).

'Ōqar, 'to get rid of unwanted persons', Heb, *'aqar*, 'to uproot', 'to get rid of', (Ben-Jacob, *Hebrew and Aramaic*, 154).

'Ōqaṣ, 'to hinder and complicate matters', 'to act like a thorn', Heb, *'Ōqéṣ*, 'thorn', (Gīl, 177).

'Ōraḍ, 'to become wide' < *'urḍ*, 'width' or < *'ārḍa*, 'to object', (Sām, 190).

'Ōraq, more commonly *ta'awraqa*, CA, 'to become rooted' < *'irq*, 'deep root', or < *'arīq*, 'deeply rooted', CA, not common (EB, 762[62]).

Qōṭagh, *qōṭar*, 'to become smelly' (pleasant or unpleasant), (Bak, 400).

'Ōtal, 'to carry s.th. heavy' < CA, *'atlā*, 'heavy', (Bak, 346).

'Osaj, 'to stretch one's neck while walking' < *'asaja*, 'same', (*Muḥīṭ*, 702).

Bōghar, 'to go' (Mosul), (Oussani, 114[63]).

62 El Said Badawi, et al., *Modern Written Arabic: A Comprehensive Grammar* (New York 2004), (henceforth EB).

63 Gabriel Oussani, 'The Arabic Dialect of Baghdad', *Journal of the American Oriental Society* 22 (1901), 97–114 (henceforth Oussani).

Bōhar, 'to be changed' (colour), 'to predict the weather', (Ḥana, *al-Alfāẓ*, 52).

Bōqar, 'to make s.th. asymmetrical', (Bak, 94), *mbōqar*, 'asymmetrical item', (Bak, 452).

Bōkar, *baykar*, 'to make a circle of s.th.', (Shīr, 20).

Bōraḥ, 'to run away', Heb, *baraḥ* (Ben-Jacob, *Hebrew and Aramaic*, 30).

Bōram, CA, *bawram*, 'to eat, gnaw', (Ghanīmah, 267); 'to turn' (intr.), 'to deceive', (DH, *Qāmūs*, 49); 'to twist' (thread, rope, moustache), (YD, *Sefat*, 111), CA, 'same'.

Bōraq < *būrāq*, 'to coat a wall with white plaster', Per, *borāq*, plaster', Lat., *burak* (Bak, 94); 'to shine', CA, *baraqa* (TA, 14).

Bōṭal, 'to be without work, idle', < *bāṭil*, 'unemployed', *bōṭal 'alā*, 'to deceive' < .

Bōzagh, 'to cause to fail', 'to spoil s.th.' (an agreement) < Tur, *buzuk* , 'crumpled', 'wrinkled', 'destroyed' (fig.), (Baz, 30).

Nōkhar, 'to decay' < *nakhara*, 'to be eaten by worms' (tree), (Cha, *Kalimāt*, 168).

Çōlaq, 'to become worn out', *mçōlaq*, 'absent-minded', 'lazy', (Gīl, 248; YD, *Sefat*, 89).

Dhōbal, 'to wither'< *dhabala*.

Dhōbaq, 'to taste', (Cha, *Ath*, 31), *w* > *b*, √ DhWQ.

Dōbar, 'to accompany s.o.', 'to follow' (a tradition or creed) < Arm, *dbār*, 'same', (Cha, *Ath*, 40). In backgammon, Per, *do bāreh*, 'twice', 'double twos' (dice), (Ḥana, *Mu'jam*, III, 95).

Dōla', 'to limp', (Sām, 170) < *dil'*, 'a limp'.

Dōlab, 'to sneak in quietly', (YD, *Sefat*, 208), 'to repeat o.s. like a *dūlāb* [wheel]', (Bak, 227).

Dōlash, and *dawlash*, 'to put a stripe under the belly of a horse'; 'to become weak and unbalanced', said of a drunken person, (Ḥana, *Mu'jam*, III, 108).

Dōqar, 'to stare' (at a book), 'to lower' (the head), (DH, *Qāmūs*, 113).

Dōzan, 'to put in order', (Bak, 217), 'to perform a job well,' (YD, *Sefat*, 208; Gīl, 94), < *dazzan, dawwaz* same, dissim.

Dōzan, 'to tune an instrument', (YD, *Sefat*, 208) < *dazzan* (Bak, 217), same.

Dawzana, see *dōzan* (YD, *Sefat*, 208; TA, 29, n. 1).

Fō 'ar, 'to become very hot', (Sām, 175), 'to flow quickly (water) from the mouth of the valley', (Thin, 121, n. 77), Syr, *pé'ar*, Heb, *pa'ar*, 'to open widely', 'to shout'.

Fōshal, *boshal*, 'to cook', 'to be too ripe', Syr, *fshāl* 'same', (FM, 432).

Gōbal, 'to mix', Heb, *gabal*, 'same'; 'to depart in a hurry', (al-Karmilī, *Majmū'ah*, I, 122, n. 51; II, 121, n. 6, 226, n. 29); *gōzal*, < Arm, *gāwzālā*, 'same', (Cha, *Ath*, 78).

Ḥōlaṣ, 'to steal a look', (Gīl, 72; YD, *Sefat*, 220).

Hōjal, 'to expel', (Mac, I, 421; Sām, 182; Bak, 501), 'to drive away s.o.', (Mac, I, 416; O'Leary, 85) < *jāla*, √ JWL, 'to expel', (Wood, 477; Thin, 277) < *hajala*, CA, 'to march', *thōjal*, 'to be driven out and become homeless', (Bak, 136; Mac, I, 432).

Ḥōmā, 'to circle', (Mac, II, 476; Erwin, *A Short Reference*, 79), 'to go around', (Ḥana, *Mu'jam*, II, 427).

Ḥōrab, (Jawād, 115) , 'to chant slogans before going to war'. This verb is attested in Kuwait too, (Ḥana, *al-Alfāẓ*,103).

Ḥōrak, 'to go around back and forth', (Jawād, 115[64]).

Ḥōran , 'to be stubborn'< *ḥiran*, IA (Ḥana, *Mu'jam*, II, 358).

Jō'ar, 'to bray' < *ja'ara* , CA, 'to shout loudly', (Ḥajj, II, 80]) < Arm, *g'ar*, (Cha, *Ath*, 31).

Jōbar, ('Awwād, 23), 'to force' < *jabara* CA, 'same', 'to imitate Jābir'.

Jōhar, 'to glare', 'to clean and polish like a diamond', (Ḥana, *Mu'jam*, II, 252), *itjōhar*, 'to become like a *jawhar* (a diamond, a substance)', (Shīr, 40).

Jōlaq, 'to open the mouth widely when speaking', 'to eat a lot in a hurry' < *jalwaqa*, 'to open a sack', (al-Karmilī, *Majmū'ah*, II, 136, n. 10); 'to laugh a lot', (Cha, *Kalimāt*, 50).

Jōmar, 'to polish, shine', (Ḥajj, II, 252), *jamrah*, 'live coal'.

Jōrāb, and *jawrab* (tr.), 'to put stockings on' (Sām, 187), CA, 'same', (Wright, I, 47[65]), Per, *jūrāb*.

Khōbaq, (tr.) and *kharbaq*, 'to twist, intertwine', (thread), (Cha, *Ath*, 37), 'to complicate matters', 'to mess up', (Bak, 200); 'to twist' (string) < Arm, *mékharbōqéh*, 'same', (YM II, *Aramaic-Kurdish*, 259).

Khōrad, *tkhōrad*, 'to be generous', (Ḥana, *Mu'jam*, II, 44), Per, *khōrandān*', 'to feed', 'to give drinks and food'.

Khōraṭ, 'to talk nonsense' < *khiraṭ* (Wood, 132) or < *kharīṭ* (CA) 'rubbish'.

Kōdhab, 'to lie' < *kawdhaba*, CA, 'same', (Mac, I, 417).

Kōfar, *kufar*, 'to be irreligious, an infidel', Heb, *kafar*, 'same', (Wood, 407; Ben-Jacob, *Hebrew and Aramaic* 90), *kifar*, 'same', (Wood, 407), *kafara*, CA.

Kōjal, 'to be haughty', Tur, *kōj*, 'stubborn', (Tikritī, VI, 110[66]).

---

64 Muṣṭafā Jawād, 'al-Lughah al-'Āmmiyyah al-'Irāqiyyah', *Lisān al-'Arab*, (Baghdad Year 8, 1933), 115–17, (henceforth Jawād).

65 William Wright, *A Grammar of the Arabic Language*[3] (Cambridge 1976), (henceforth Wright).

66 'Abd al-Raḥmān al-Tikrītī, *Jamharat al-Amthāl al-Baghdādiyyah* VI (Baghdad 1991), (henceforth Tikritī, VI).

Kōlaḥ, 'to get s.o. in trouble', (Bak, 426), *tkōlaḥ*, 'to be in trouble unexpectedly', (Cha, *Kalimāt*, 41), fig.), (Thin, 104; Bak, 426).

Lōhaj, 'to be enflamed' < *wahaja*, CA, 'to glare'; 'to blaze', (DH, *Qāmūs*, 251).

Hawzar 'alā, 'to be angry at', (DH, *Qāmūs*, 91).

Lō'aṭ, 'to beat a lot', 'to burn', 'to torture', < CA, *la'aṭa* (Thin, 191, n. 48), Arm, *lé'aṭah*, 'to lick'.

Mōdhar, 'to become rotten' < *madhira*, CA, 'same', (DH, *Qāmūs*, 274).

Mōlas, 'to be worn out and smooth' (threads of a screw), (Erwin, *A Short Reference*, 78), 'to become hairless', (Jawād, 115) < *amlas*, 'hairless face and body', *immōlas*, 'an epithet for a penniless person', (Shāl, III, 136).

Mōsar, *tmōsar*, 'to turn over s.o.', (Ben-Jacob, *Hebrew and Aramaic*, 104), Heb, *masar*, 'to hand over'; 'to say ethical words', 'to behave ethically', Heb, *mūsār*, 'ethics', (Ṭobī, 77, Avīshūr, 204).

Mōshaḥ, 'to anoint' < *mashaḥ*, Arm, 'oil', (Cha, *Ath*, 83).

Nō 'ar, 'to bray a lot', *na'ara*, CA; Arm, *né'arah*, (YM I, *Hebrew-Aramaic*, 322).

Nō'af, Heb, *na'af*, 'to commit adultery', (Avīshūr, 226).

Nōqal, 'to transfer' (tr.), (Sām, 188; Naqqāsh, *Nzūlah*, 157) < CA, *nāqala*.

Paswal, 'to wither', (Cha, *Kalimāt*, 32), *mpaswir* (fig.) 'good for nothing', 'obsolete'; (Ḥana, *Mu'jam*, III, 41), '*pasūl*', Heb, 'same' < Per, *pazūlidan*, 'to wither'.

Pōqar, 'to make s.o. a heretic', Heb, *tpōqar*, 'to become a heretic', (Gīl, 206).

Pōsaq, or *bōsāq*, 'to be infected with *bāsūq*' (a type of insect which lives in wheat flour), (Bak, 64).

Qōbal, *tqōbal*, 'to agree unwillingly', used by Iraqi Jews (Avīshūr, 227), *qabila*, 'same', CA.

Qōfal, 'to lock', *qafala*, CA, 'same'.

Qōla', 'to gouge the eye', Shīr < *qala'a*, 'to uproot', CA, 'same', 'to perish', (al-Karmilī, *Dīwān*, 104[67]), *tqōla'*, 'to be uprooted', (Ḥana, *Mu'jam*, II, 90), 'to cast in a *qālab* (a mould)', (TA, 54).

Qōlaj, 'to have stomach ache', < *Qōlanj*, 'internal illness', (*Muḥīṭ*, 763).

Qōlab, 'to pour in a mould' < *qālab*, Sām, 190); in Yemen, 'to cover with leather'.

Qōna', 'to convince' < *qawna'a* < *qanna'a*, CA, 'same'.

---

67 Anastas Mārī al-Karmilī, *Dīwān al-Tiftāf, aw Ḥikāyāt Baghdādiyyah*[2] (Baghdad 2000), (henceforth al-Karmilī, *Dīwān*).

Qōqaz, (ʿAwwād, 24), 'to put s.th. in an unstable place', hence 'to shake', (Bak, 400); in the Lebanese dialect, 'to sit with difficulty', (AF, *Mu'jam*, 146); 'same' in the Jewish dialect.

Rōbaṣ, *rabaṣa*, 'to sink to the bottom of s.th. like in a glass of water', (AF, *Mu'jam*, 62).

Rōbaṣ, or *rawbaṣ*, 'to clean' (silver) (DH, *Qāmūs*, 125), 'to wring' (clothes after washing them), *rbāṣ*, Syr (AF, *Mu'jam*, 68).

Rōkaḍ wara, 'to run after s.o. continuously', (Ḥana, *Mu'jam*, III, 199) < *rakaḍa*, 'to run'.

Rahban, 'to make s.o. a monk', (Shīr, 74), Syr. < *Rāhib*, 'monk', CA.

Sawkar, 'to smoke a cigarette' (*sighārah*), (DH, *Qāmūs*, 144).

Shōbak, 'to flatten', 'to knead', Per, *shōbāq*, 'roller', (Bak, 303; MM; 214; TA, 45; Shīr, 4).

Shōbāsh, 'to give gratitude' < Per, Tur, and Kur, 'gratitude', *shōbāsh*, 'money given to musicians on happy occasions'. Originally it was a Syriac word, *shōbūsh*, which refers to the production of grains given to government employees when inspecting farms (Thin, 100; Cha, *Kalimāt*, 125).

Shōḥad, 'to bribe', Heb, 'same'.

Shōghath, 'to be worm eaten', (Gīl, 130; YD, *Sefat*, 47).

Shōḥar, 'to become black', (AF, *Mu'jam*, 90); 'to blacken with soot' < *shaḥḥara*, and *shaḥwara*, dissim. - *ḥḥ* - > - *ḥw*, CA, 'same', or > *shiḥār*, 'soot', (DH, *Qāmūs*, 51). Hebrew has it as *shiḥḥér* < *shaḥōr*, 'black', Syr, *shōḥārā* (FM, 271), used in the sense of being embarrassed (Avīshūr, 228). It is attested in the Lebanese dialect as *shaḥbar*, 'to blacken', (AF, *Mu'jam*, 101). *Shaḥbar*, see *shaḥtar* in AF, *Mu'jam*, 90.

Shōkhag, or *shōkhar*, 'to have an acid taste and a sharp smell in the throat', (Bak, 303); 'to snore', (Wood, 251; Ḥajj, V, 347). In the Jewish dialect in Baghdad and Mosul, it means 'to get drunk', 'to drink *shékhar*', Heb, 'wine', (Rabīn, 154; YD, *Sefat*, 149; Avishur, 229).

Shōlaq, 'to boil', 'to cook', 'to scrape off' < Arm, *shlāq*, 'to boil', 'to collapse' (wall), 'to destroy' < *shallaqa*, CA, dissim. *-ll-* > *-wl-*, *tshōlaq*, 'to be afflicted with inflammation and redness in the thighs and armpit due to heat', (Cha, *Ath*, 60); 'to wrap o.s.', (Bak, 122).

Shōrab, 'to cut the moustache'.

Shalfaṭ, (ʿAwwād, 24), 'to get hold of s.th.', 'to climb with difficulty', (Piamenta, I, 265); 'to be ulcerated in the mouth because of eating piquant seasonings'; CA, same, but also it means 'to be turbid' (water).

Ṣōfar and *ṣawfar*, 'to whistle' < *ṣafara*, 'same', (Mac, II, 421; Erwin, *A Short Reference*, 79; DH, *Qāmūs*, 168).

Ṣōjal, 'to be convicted', Tur, *ṣūç*, 'crime', (Tikritī, VI, 110).

Ṣōpar, Arm, 'to be indifferent to s.o.'< *sappar*, 'to take care of one's own self', said to insult s.o. (Bak, 273). Originally the verb is Aramaic *saybar*, 'to take', 'to buy', 'to contain', ('Ubaydī, 96; Baz, 96).

Ṣōrab, and *sōrab*, 'to become dim' (sight), (Cha, *Ath*, 61; Baz, 103; Wood, 229; 'Ubaydī, 52); Arm, *ṣwārā*, 'darkness', 'blindness', or *ṣwār*, 'to become blurred' (vision); (Bak, 213; al-Karmilī, *Majmū'ah*, I, 212, n. 25), *tṣōrab*, 'to be blurry' (eyes), a variation of which is *tṣōrig* in Mārdīn north of Mosul, (FJ, 160[68]).

Ṭōḥal, 'to be afflicted with an enlarged spleen'.

Ṭōbaz, 'to lower the head and stick out one's buttock', (Thin, 78; YD, *Sefat*, 223; Gīl, 157).

Ṭōla', 'to leak puss', (Naqqāsh, *Nzūlah*, 54); 'to be enflamed', (Ḥajj, I, 60; Jawād, 115). It is attested in the Kuwaiti dialect and in Basra (Ḥana, *al-Alfāẓ*, 379).

Ṭōṭaḥ, 'to win in wrestling', √ ṬWH (Gīl, 157), *imṭōṭaḥ*, 'to be unbalanced when walking', (Ḥana, *Mu'jam*, II, 73 'Ubaydī, 48); 'one who wobbles as a result of being drunk', (Bak, 327) < *aṭāḥa*, CA, 'to toss to the ground'; (Shīr, 90). *Carkhal*, 'to spin' (the *l* is an infix), < *çirakh*, 'to turn on a lathe', (Wood, 84).

Zōghal, 'to cheat', 'to steal and hide the theft', (YD, *Sefat*, 162), *zéghalah*. This verb is attested in the Kuwaiti dialect as well (Ḥana, *al-Alfāẓ*, 163).

Zōzā, Kur, 'to become very hot', (Bak, 254).

Some of the quadriliteral verbs in the *féal* Form originated from intransitive triradical verbs, but some have a causative meaning, like *nézal* < *anzala*, CA, 'to bring down' and *ṭela'*, 'to bring out' or 'to make s.o. go out' < *ṭalla'*, 'to take out'.

Elam, 'to inform'< *'alima*, CA, 'to know', (Kāmil, 36).

'Eqal, 'to cause s.o. to reason', *t'éqal*, 'to be fussy', 'to pretend to be wise', said sarcastically, (Ḥana, *Mu'jam*, II, 80; Shāl, II, 322).

'Eshiq, 'to be in love with', (Gīl, 168).

Bé'ad, 'to send away', 'to dismiss'.

Béhaḍ, 'to pick a quarrel', 'to be stubborn', (Bak, 99).

Bérakh, 'to bless', (Ben-Jacob, *Hebrew and Aramaic*, 30), Heb, *bérékh*, 'same'.

---

68 W. Fischer and O. Jastro, *Handbuch der arabischen Dialecte* (Wiesbaden 1980), (henceforth FJ).

Béraq, 'to shine'< *baraqa*, 'same'.

Béṭar, 'to shoe' (an animal), 'to practice the veterinary art of furriery', CA, 'same'. This verb is attested also in Palestine and Syria, (Driver, 78).

Démag, 'to be stuck' (eyebrows), but *dammaqa*, CA, means the opposite, 'to add flour to prevent sticking', (Ḥana, *Mu'jam*, III, 84), dissim. *-mm- > ém*.

Déwar, 'to turn left or right', (Ḥana, *Mu'jam*, III, 102; Erwin, *A Short Reference*, 79), 'to turn around', (Wood, 173).

Céwar, 'to whip s.o. on the soles of his feet and beat him', (Ḥana, *Mu'jam*, II, 318). In Kuwait this verb means, 'to make a u-turn', (ibid.).

Fésagh, 'to oppose', 'to be stubborn', (Bak, 363).

Féshal, 'to be weak and lazy', CA, *fashila*, 'same', (*Muḥīṭ*, 691).

Gélaḥ, 'to be afflicted with tetanus, or with dryness and shrinking of the body', (Cha, *Ath*, 76).

Gézar and *çézar*, (Christians in Mosul), 'to be ripe or cooked insufficiently', (lentils or beans, because the skins of beans shrink and harden when they are cooked and look like the skin of a hedgehog, Arm, *qazzūrah*, (Cha, *Ath*, 29).

Ghéhab, 'to become dark', (al-Karkhī, *Dīwān*, III, 382[69]) < CA, 'to disappear'.

Ghélaṭ, 'to cause a mistake on purpose' < *gallaṭa*, CA, 'same', or *ghaliṭa*, 'to make a mistake'.

Ghéqan, 'to make s.o. cry a lot', 'to make s.o. miserable', (YD, *Sefat*, 177), *tghéqan*, 'to be pale and unconscious', (Gīl, 39).

Hérab, 'to run away', (Gīl, 971) < *haraba*, CA, 'same'.

Ḥéshak, 'to crowd another person' < *ḥashaka*, CA, 'same', (Bak, 17).

Ḥéwad, 'to deceive' < *ḥāwada*, CA, or *ḥāda*, 'to stray', (Bak, 184).

Ka'ka', 'to tear', (al-Karkhī, *Dīwān*, III, 382, n. 1).

Khélaṣ, 'to separate two quarrelling persons', hence, 'to rescue', *khallṣa* (Bak, 202), dissim. *-ll- > -él-*.

Khéwaz, 'to be stubborn', (Bak, 203), 'to deceive', ('Ubaydı, 48).

Médan, more commonly *tmédan* and *tmadyan* (neologism), 'to become civilized'< *tmaddana*, CA, 'same', (Ḥana, *Mu'jam*, II, 117; EB, 744), sometimes said sarcastically (Mac, II, 434).

Mélakh, 'to run away' < *malakha*, CA, 'same', (MM, 314).

---

69 'Abbūd al-Karkhī, *Dīwān al-Karkhī* III (Baghdad 1967), (henceforth al-Karkhī, *Dīwān*).

Méran and *mayran*, 'to fasten', (DH, *Qāmūs*, 277).

Néwash, 'to hand over'< *nāwash*, IA, 'same', (Bak, 490).

Qé'ad, 'to seat' < *qa'ada*, 'to sit'

Qébi', 'to crouch', (Gīl, 209) < *qaba'a*, CA, 'same'.

Qégaj, 'to twist' (tr.), 'to bend', *mqégaj*, 'twisted', (Gīl, 223).

Séghaj, 'to become like sesame oil', < CA *sarij*, 'sesame oil' (Baghdadi Jews).

Séraf or *saryaf*, 'to become wet' < *ṣarifa*, CA, 'overflow' (water), (Sām, 165).

Ṣébaḥ, 'to become morning' < *aṣbaḥa*, CA, 'same'.

Séṭar, *sayṭara 'alā*, 'to control', (Erwin, *A Short Reference*, 78), CA, 'same'.

Shélakh, 'to leave alone', 'to flee', (Ḥana, *Fiqh*, 66; MM, 215), 'to make a noise like the humming of bees', Arm, *shalakh*.

Shémaṣ, 'to dart away', (Mac, I, 416) < *shammaṣa*, 'to expel', dissim. *-mm-* > *-ém-* (Sām, 168), 'to sneak out', (Ḥana, *Fiqh*, 66).

Shéqal, 'to weigh'. This verb is attested in Hebrew as well, *shaqal*, 'same', Arm, *shqal*, (Cha, *Ath*, 58).

Shéqaṣ, 'to be high on one side and low on another due to shrinkage' (dress), (Bak, 305).

Shéréz, 'to stitch together', 'to sew a border around the edge of a garment', (Wood, 254; Baz, 111), CA, *shéraza*, 'same', (MM, 428), *shérāzéh* (YM I, *Hebrew-Aramaic*, 387).

Ṭéla', 'to raise', ('Awwād, 23).

Témar, ('Awwād, 23), 'to bandage', 'to nurse' < *tīmār*, Per, 'care, attendance', (Cha, *Kalimāt*, 46).

Zébaq, 'to become sticky and wet', <*zi'baq*, (Shīr, 76).

Zédal, 'to add', 'to increase', 'to become like Zayd', (Kāmil, 17).

As for quadriliteral verbs in *fa'lā* (Form I), they exist in the dialects of North Africa, Zanzibar, Oman, Mosul and most of the Arabic dialects in Ethiopia (Kāmil, 13).

The *fa'lā* type is very rare in IA. I found only two verbs, which are derived from common nouns: *dahdā*, 'to roll down' (tr.) < *dihidwānah*, 'a slope', (Wood, 167); *ma'fā* ('Awwād, 25) , 'to recover', *'āfiyah*, 'health'.

B. 2.5. Type 1. ', or B, L, M, H, N, R, T, 3.4

In the following verbs, the infixes are in bold fonts, and the verbs are arranged alphabetically. Some of them are borrowed:

*'A**k**mash*, 'to frown a little', (Turj, 101) < CA, *'akasha*, 'to frown'.

Ba'laṣ, 'to eat a lot of fruit', (Cha, 20, Arm, *blaṣ*); 'to chew', 'to pave', (Bak, 85).

Ba'thar, 'to scatter', (Wood, 39; Ḥana, *Mu'jam*, I, 547), dissim. of *badhdhar*, *-dhdh-* > *-'dh-* > *ba'dhar* > *ba'thar*.

Bahdar, 'to squander', (DH, *Qāmūs*, 48) < *badhdhara*, 'to scatter', dissim. *-dhdh-* > *-hdh-*, and *bahdhar* > *bahdar* (*dh* > *d*).

Da'thar, 'to ignore taking care of o.s. and look bad', <*dathar*, 'dirt', (Sām, 70).

Damlaj, 'to enter s.th. and be deeply rooted', CA, 'to become round and fat', *mdamlaj*, 'compact', (Gīl, 245; YD, *Sefat*, 120).

Falḥam, 'to be dehydrated', (Sām, 174), 'to be dry (tongue, throat) because of thirst', (Bak, 369; Thin, 116), < *faḥḥama*, 'to be still' (water).

Falgaḥ, more commonly *tfalgaḥ*, 'to turn one's back when sitting or laughing', (Thin, 117).

Falṭaḥ, see *farṭaḥ* (*r* > *l*).

Galfa', *ghalfa'*, 'to be dry and wrinkled' (leather, skin) < *qaffa'a* > *-ff-* > *-lf-*, *qalfa'a* > *qarfa'*, *l* > *r*, 'to shrink or dry because of cold or fear'; (Bak, 391; Gīl, 216; Sām, 176); 'to be dirty', (Shāl, 504, III) < *garfū'ah*, 'a small piece of dirt in the nose', 'to become old' (fig.), (YD, *Sefat*, 186), 'to pile items in disorder', (Gīl, 59), *gabal*, Heb, 'to mix'.

Ḥalfaṣ, ('Awwād, 23), 'to spread one's legs apart', (Bak, 359), 'to be able to break free from s.o.'s grip', (Sām, 157; Ḥana, *Mu'jam*, II, 400), *tḥalfaṣ*, 'to move o.s.'; (DH, *Qāmūs*, 56), < LFS or FLS. The expression *maku tḥilfiṣ tfilfuṣ*, 'there is no way out', is said to a desperate person who can't get away from his troubles (Ḥana, *Mu'jam*, II, 400); *ḥafaṣa* > *faḥaṣa*), CA, 'to kick the ground with the legs in order to be free'. The expression *faḥaṣa birijlihi*, CA, 'he kicked the ground with his leg' may explain that the *l* is an infix, and *faḥaṣa* > *ḥafaṣa*, or *falfaṣa*.

Hamdagh/r, 'to make a sound from the nostrils like *hadīr* (the surging of the sea)', (Bak, 506; 'to mutter', DH, *Qāmūs*, 293).

Ḥanjal, 'to jump up and down on one foot', 'to bounce'; 'to shoe' (a horse), (Wood, 483) < *ḥajala*, 'same', dissim. *-jj-* > *-nj-* (Sām, 183; Thin, 287), CA, *jaljal*, or < *zangūl*, Per, 'a small bell', (Cha, *Kalimāt*, 52), *tḥanjal*, 'to be haughty', (DH, *Qāmūs*, 57).

Ḥatraf, more commonly *tḥatraf*, 'to behave improperly', 'to incite one against the other', (Sām, 156).

Ḥatrash, 'to provoke s.o.', (Sām, 156).

Jal'aṭ, 'to annoy, disturb' < Syr, *ja'ṭa*, 'same'.

La'baṭ, 'to flop', (fish or hen after slaughtering), Arm, *méla'boṭé*, (YM I, *Hebrew-Aramaic*, 264). In CA, *labaṭa* means 'to strike'.

Ganṭar, *qanṭar*, 'to drop s.o. from a horse or a high place' < *qaṭṭara*, dissim. *ṭṭ* > *nṭ* (Thin, 178); *tganṭar*, 'to fall from a horse' (epithet), (Ḥana, *Mu'jam*, II, 99; al-Karmilī, *Majmū'ah*, II, 103, n. 10; MM, 160). Note the saying, *illī mā-yitganṭar mā yiṣir khayyāl*, 'he who does not fall from the horse does not become a knight', (Shāl, I, 210), implying that experiences and difficulties create wise people.

Salqaṭ, 'to cause to fall, drop', (Sām, 166), < *saqaṭa*, CA, 'to fall', 'to accuse s.o. by saying s.th. untrue' (*ṣallaṭ*), (Gīl, 115), but if the root is √ LQṬ, 'to collect', then the *ṣ* is a prefix (Ben-Jacob, *Hebrew and Aramaic*, 98) (Baghdadi Jews).

Ṭambaz, 'to shrink out of fear or cold', (Gīl, 156; YD, *Sefat*, 164) < *ṭabaza*, CA, 'to sit coiled'.

Za'maṭ < *zumaṭ*, 'to boast', (Wood, 206; YD, *Sefat*, 113).

Zablaṭ, and *zalbṭ*, 'to peel', 'to remove' (especially hair from the head), *tzablaṭ*, 'to slip' 'to slip away' (fish), (Ḥana, *Mu'jam*, III, 255; Mac, II, 548; Bak, 120). It may also mean 'to swallow without chewing the food' < *zalaṭ* (YD, *Sefat*, 39).

Zaḥlaq/g, 'to cause to slide, roll', (Mac, I, 425; YD, *Sefat*, 218; Wood, 202), 'to roll on a slippery surface', 'to lead astray', '*zaḥlagah bi-l-ḥaçī*', 'he led s.o. to say s.th. he did not want to', (Bak, 237), *tzaḥlag*, 'to slip' (intr.), (Mac, I, 432).

Zamjar, 'to rage, scold', *zajara*, CA, 'same'.

Hamdar, 'to be angry', 'to roar' (ocean); √ HDR.

B. 2. Quadriradical Verbs Resulting from Triradical Verbs Augmented Externally by Adding an Infix after the Second Radical of the Triliteral Verbs

B. 2.6. Type 1.2. M. 4.

Ja'mar, 'to shape s.th. round sloppily', (Ḥana, *Mu'jam*, II, 213; Sām, 155) 'to talk nonsense' (fig.) < *jam'ara* (metathesis); 'to bray', Heb, *ga'ar*, 'to shout', *mja'mar*, 's.th. unshaped well', (Wood, 73).

La'maṭ, 'to lick', (Bak, 264), *la'aṭa*, CA.

Ṣalma', 'to make bald', (Ḥana, *al-Alfāẓ*, 222; Sām, 169), *aṣla'*, 'bald'.

B. 2.7 Type. 1.2 . W. 4

The infix *w* after the second radical of the root may be a secondary development. Examples from IA:

'Ajwagh, 'to make s.th. in an unequal proportion in form and distance', (Bak, 334).

La'wak, see *'alwak*.

'Alwak, 'to have a speech impediment', 'to speak as if one is chewing gum' < *'ilk*, 'mastic', (Bak, 343), or < *'alaka*. The *w* is an infix.

'Anwath, 'to become sad or lazy', 'to be humble', < Heb, *'anaw*, 'humble, modest', used by Baghdadi Jews, *m'anwith*, 'sad', 'absent-minded', (Gīl, 249).

'Arwaj < 'to hamper', 'to do an incomplete job' < *'awwaja*, 'to bend', 'to twist', (Sām, 171), dissim. *-ww-* > *-rw-*.

'Athwal, 'to sully', (Sām, 170), 'to become smoky' < distortion of *'athwan* < *'uthān*, 'smoke', (Thin, 82).

'Atwan 'to become dark and gloomy' because of clouds, wind and thunder √ 'TM. (*m* > *n*), (Bak, 333).

Baḥwash, ('Awwād), 'to dig with one finger', (Sām, 152) < *baḥatha*, 'to search', where *th* > *sh*. It is attested in the Syrian and Lebanese dialects (AF, *Mu'jam*, 6; Driver, 77), Heb, *baḥash*, 'to stir' (tea), Arm, *békhashā*.

Bathwal, *pathwal*, ('Awwād, 22), 'to do or say s.th. incorrectly', (Bak, 102).

Da'wash, 'to quarrel', (Bak, 221), 'to become dark', CA.

Ḍajwar, 'to be annoyed' < 'to be bored'< *aḍjara*, CA, 'same', (Sām, 170; Dabb, 136; al-Karmilī, II, *Majmū'ah*, II, 350, n. 26).

Ga'waṭ, 'to be in pain', 'to eat with the hands in a repulsive way', Syr, *g'aṭ* (FM, 103).

Hajwal, *hawjal*, 'to expel', (Mac, 421; Sām, 182; Bak, 501; Thin, 277), *thawjal*, *thajwal*, 'to be driven out and become homeless', (Bak, 136; Mac, I, 416).

Harwal, 'to jog', (Sām, 183).

'Atbar < distortion of CA, *i'tabar*, where the initial *hamzah* is deleted, 'to consider', 'to respect', (Sām, 171).

Jarwan, 'to moan loudly', (al-Karmilī, *Majmū'ah*, I, 62, n. 20).

Karwan, 'to beat', (MM, 263), as in *akal karwān* and *karwanūh*, 'he was beaten badly', 'he took a beating', (Sām, 191; Shāl, II, 542; Dabb, 142).

Kharbaṭ, 'to descend from a pole or a tree' *kharaṭa*, 'to hold s.th., when going down from a tree' < *khūṭ*, 'a branch'; 'to eat voraciously', (DH, *Qāmūs*, 248); 'to sully', 'to squander', 'to throw in disorder', (Ḥana, *Mu'jam*, II, 104); 'to cut branches off trees', *kharbaṭa* (Sām, 160); *tkharwaṭ*, 'to tie a rope in order to descend from a tree or a pole', (Hajj, *Baghdādiyyāt* III, 178, n. 79).

Kharwaṭ, 'to talk nonsense', *khiraṭ*, 'to wipe out', (Wood, 132; Ḥana, *Mu'jam*, I, 104).

La'was, 'to chew' (food) (DH, *Qāmūs*, 248), Syr *l'as*, CA *la'asa*. In the language of the villagers, 'to sally'.

La'wash, 'to be stingy', 'to cause pain by abstaining from helping others who are in dire need' (Gīl, 238).

La'waṭ, 'to cause pain', 'to be hit by a stick repeatedly', (Thin, 191), 'to burn s.o. on the neck', 'to lick', (Shāl, II, 80).

Lahwaq, 'to say s.th. incorrectly and quickly', 'to do sloppy work', (Bak, 449) < *lawwaja*, 'to twist', (Sām, 181), dissim. *-ww-* > *-hw-*; 'to walk fast at a variable speed', < *lahwaj* > *lahwaq*, *j* > *q* (Thin, 202).

Na'waṣ, 'to be discontent and angry', 'to pretend to cry' (like a dog) < *na'wīṣ*, 'the sound of a puppy', (Bak, 486; 'Ubaydī, 54; Thin, 246), 'to howl' (puppy) < Arm, *'waṣ*, 'to cry', (Cha, *Ath*, 86).

Marwaj, *tmarwaj*, 'to sway', (Sām, 181).

Na'waj, 'to croak' (raven) < *na'aja*, 'same'.

Na'wash, *tna'wash*, 'to recover from sickness', 'to be refreshed', (Thin, 246).

Naghwash, 'to cause an itching or tickling sensation' (ants), (Thin, 246), 'to make s.o. miserable' < *naghghash*, 'to disturb', (Wood, 464), dissim. *-gg-* > *-gw-*.

Naqwar, 'to make a hole' < *naqara*, 'to prick', *nuqrah*, 'hole', 'hollow'.

Naqwash, < *naqasha*, CA, 'to mark with speckles', or 'to make a lot of holes', √ NQB, (*b* > *w*) (Sām, 182).

Naṣwal, ('Awwād, 25) < *naṣala*, 'to fall off' (hair, feathers), (Wehr, 971).

Pa'war, 'to open wide'< CA, 'same', 'to bend the head', (DH, *Qāmūs*, 112).

Qaḥwar, 'to trim the edges in order to make a circle', 'to cut a hole in cloth' < *qawwara*, CA, (Sām, 175; Thin, 159), dissim. *qawwar* where *-ww-* > *ḥw*.

Qaḥwaṭ, 'to nibble', 'to gnaw' < Arm, *qéraṭah*, 'to cut with one's teeth', (YM I, *Hebrew-Aramaic*, 401).

Qashwal, 'to peel off skin' < Arm, *qshā*, 'to wipe one's face', 'to steal', (Sām, 177), as in *gashwalūhum il- ḥarāmiyyah*, 'the thieves cleaned them out', (Thin, 167).

Qalwaṭ, *galwaṭ*, 'to cause pain', (Sām, 177; Thin, 176; Baz, 23). Note the expression *sha'waṭnī w-qalwaṭnī*, 'he caused me pain', (lit, 'he burned and fried me' [fig.]), (Baz, 23), Arm, *shyāṭ*, 'smell of burnt food', (Bak, 287), √ ShWṬ.

Shar'aṭ, 'to tear into pieces' < *ra'aṭ*, CA, 'to tear fabric or skin', (Sām, 163; 'Ubaydī, 48).

Saqwa', 'to become weak and thin'; *mṣaqwa'*, 'frail', (Ḥana, *al-Alfāẓ*, 351).

Sarwaṭ, 'to scratch', Arm, *saraṭa*, (Sām, 165).

Salwa', 'to become frail and thin', *msalwi'*, 'feeble', (Baghdad), (Ḥana, *al-Alfāẓ*, 173, 351; Shāl, III, 78).

Saqwa' see *salwa'* above.

Shalwaṭ, 'to scorch' (food), (Wood, 252), dissemination of *shawwaṭ*, *ww* > *lw*, 'to become upset and disturbed'. Syr, *lhiṭ*, *h* >*w* for facilitating pronunciation (FM, 291); 'to anger', (Gīl, 128); 'to cause pain', (Sām, 167; YD 173).

Sharmat, 'to draw the sword', <, CA, same. The *r* is an infix.

Sha'waṭ, 'to burn', (Sām, 167); 'to scorch', (Wood, 242) < Arm, *shyāṭ*, 'to cause pain', (fig.) < *shi'waṭ*, CA, 'lightly burnt', (Bak, 287).

Shawshaṭ, *shōshaṭ*, (tr.) 'to burn', (food on the bottom of a pan), (DH, *Qāmūs*, 159), figuratively, 'to make one suffer', (Shāl, II, 569).

Saqwaṭ, 'to itch between the fingers', (Bak, 269; YD, *Sefat*, 221), 'to be out of order' < *saqaṭ*, 'out of order', said about a person who has a bodily defect, or about an item which is no longer good for anything' < Arm, (YM II, *Aramaic-Kurdish*, 340); 'to lock a door with a *siqqāṭah* (locker)', ('Ubaydī, 49).

Shakhwal, 'to shed a lot of tears', (Bak, 285), 'to ooze' (water); ('Ubaydī, 54), 'to prune' < *shakhala*, 'to sieve'.

Zaghwal, 'to deceive' > *zāghal*, 'to cheat and lie', (Gīl, 102; YD, *Sefat*, 160), 'to steal and hide the theft'. Note the Jewish expression, *zaghwal il-ḥkiyyī*, 'he settled the matter' by concealing the truth, (YD, *Sefat*, 160).

Zalwaṭ, 'to get rid of s.o.', (Ḥana, *Mu'jam*, III, 256).

B. 2.8. Type 1.2. B, L, R, T, Ṭ, '. 4.

In the following examples, the bold radical indicates the infix:

*Ba'**l**aj*, ('Awwād, 22), 'to complain about a stomach ache', (Sām, 154) < *ba'aja*, 'to tear', 'to split', CA.

*Ba**ḥ**rath*, 'to crumble and scatter' < *ba'thar*, CA (Sām, 152; Ḥana, *Mu'jam*, I, 467) < *bahthara*, CA, 'same', (metathesis).

*Ba**n**baq*, 'to stare'< *banaqa*, CA, 'same', 'to enjoy others' money', (Bak, 113).

*Da'**m**ak*, ('Awwād, 23) < *da'aka* and *dalaka*, CA 'to rub, scrub', (Wehr, 282), *di'aç*, IA, 'to bump', Arm, *dé'aka*, (YM I, *Hebrew-Aramaic*, 89; Bak, 413).

*Dagh**l**aṣ*, ('Awwād, 23), 'to be furious' < *daghisa*, 'same', (*Muḥīṭ*, 383).

*Fa'**l**ak*, 'to rub s.th. in order to clean it', (Mac, II, 425).

*Har**b**aj*, 'to tear' (a book), (DH, *Qāmūs*, 292) < *harraj*, 'to be excited', CA, dissim. *-rr-* > *rb-*, HBJ, 'to scratch'.

*Fas**t**aq*, 'to cause a relapse' < *fitaq*, 'to unstitch', (fig.), Heb, *pasaq*, 'to invalidate'; < *fassaqa*, 'to interrupt s.o. talking', CA, dissim. *ss* > *st*; Syr, *fsāq*.

*Ja'**l**ak*, 'to fold carelessly', (paper); 'to wrinkle', (DH, *Qāmūs*, 78); *ja''aqa*, 'to wrinkle', dissim. *-''-* > *-'l* and *q* >*k*.

*Lagh**m**aṭ*, 'to sully', (Sām, 180), 'to be clamorous and noisy' < *laghaṭa*, 'same'.

Mar'aṭ, 'to pluck' < *mariṭa*, CA, 'same', or < *ma'aṭa*, 'to pluck'. The *r* is an infix or it is a composition of *laghama+ghamaṭa*.

*Ma**l**ghaṭ*, see *laghmaṭ*.

*Nagh**m**ash*, 'to wish to get s.th.', usually used in the expression *naghmash qalbu*, (Mosul), 'he desired' (lit. 'his heart desired'), (Bak, 487), *naghasha*, 'same'.

Nahṭar, 'to breath quickly due to fatigue' < *nihaṭ*, t > *ṭ*.

Nakraz, 'to prick' < *nakkaza*, 'to jump up and down', (Wood, 469), dissim. *-kk-* > *kr-*.

Qal'aṭ, 'to sully' < *qallaṭa*, CA, dissim. *-ll-* > *-l'-* (DH, *Qāmūs*, 226) < Syr, *lqaṭ*, 'to be stingy and act as if one is in dire need', (FM, 460).

Shamrakh, 'to be very tall, high' < *shamakha*, CA, 'same' (the *r* is an infix); 'to peel a cluster of unripe dates or grapes' < *shamrūkh*, 'a cluster of grapes or unripe dates', CA, (*Muḥīṭ*, 401). *Sharmakh*, 'to do s.th. carelessly', (Cha, *Ath*, 56; Ṭobī, 42).

Shantaf, 'to wear earnings', CA, 'to make scornful gestures with the nose', (Gīl, 125) < *shannaf*, dissim. *-nn-* > *-nt-*, 'to cause joy', as in *shannafa asmā'anā*, CA, 'he entertained us', (Bak, 303), 'to become short' (dress), (Sām, 168).

*Ṭar**b**aq*, *ṭar**b**ag*, 'to bang', 'to make irritating sounds', *ṭaraqa*, CA, 'same'; 'to hurry', (MM, 220). It is likely that the Baghdadis derived the verb *ṭarbag* from the Persian *ṭarbāgah*, ‘a place of joy, fun’; in the Yemenite dialect, ‘to threaten loudly’, (Piamenta, II, 301).

Za'baj, ‘to irritate’< *za'aja*, ‘same’, (Bak, 242).

Za'bal, ‘to act improperly and commit a folly’ (child), ‘to do unfruitful work’, *zabbala*, ‘to sully’, dissim. *-bb-* > *-'b-*, (Sām, 164), ‘to mess up’, (Ḥana, *Mu'jam*, III, 245), ‘to talk nonsense’, (Gīl, 104; YD, *Sefat*, 164).

Za'baṭ, ‘to peel’, ‘to remove’, (Bak, 145), or ‘to become short’ < *za'aṭa*, ‘to make a sound’; ‘to strangle’, (*Muḥīṭ*, 372).

Zablaq, ‘to slip’, (Bak, 236) < *zalaqa*, CA, ‘same’.

Zaḥlaf, ‘to cheat’, ‘to change s.o. from doing good to doing bad’ < *azḥafa*, ‘same’, (Ḥana, *Mu'jam*, III, 271) < *zaḥafa*, CA, ‘to advance slowly’, (Sām, 164; Wright, I, 47).

Zakhraf, ‘to adorn’ < Per, *muzakhraf*, ‘embellished speech with lies’, or *zakhafa*, ‘to show off’, (*Muḥīṭ*, 368).

B. 3. Augmentation of Triradical Verbs Externally by Adding Suffixes.[70]

B. 3.1. Type 1.2.3. M

The consonant *m* as a suffix morpheme is found in Hebrew, Ethiopian, Yemenite dialects, Tijrani and in Classical Arabic verbs, nouns and adjectives. The morpheme *m* is attested as a suffix to bi-radical and triliteral verbs in CA as shown in the following examples: *jadhima*, 'to cut one's hand', and *jadhdha*, 'to cut', *hadhrama*, 'to jabber' and *hadhara*, *zarqama*, 'to become dark blue' and *zaraqa*, 'to become blue', *dalqama* and *dalaqa*, *halsama* and *halisa*, (Sām, 148; Kāmil, 53–5; Jalal al-Din al-Suyūṭī, *al-Muzhir fī 'Ulūm al-Lughah wa-Anwā'uah*, Vol. II [Cairo 1971], 165, 166).

The following examples utilize *m* as a suffix to form quadriradical verbs in IA:

Dalham, 'to look unhappy, murky'< *daliha*, CA, 'to become gloomy, darker in the face more than the body', (Wood, 164).

Ḥaghjam, 'to cause constipation', *mḥaghjim*, 'shrunk', (Gīl, 67; YD, *Sefat*, 61).

Harjam, 'to become embarrassed', 'to be confused', < *haraja*, 'to be stubborn'. The *m* is a suffix (Sām,156; Ḥana, *Mu'jam*, II, 352); 'to return to one's own group', as in the expression, *harjamat al-'iblu*, CA, 'the camels returned to the other [camels]', CA, (Sām, 156); 'to bleed', (YD, *Sefat*, 259) √ HJM. The *r* is an infix.

Haṣram, *ḥarmaṣ*, 'to be caught between the nail and the skin of the finger' (blood), (Sām, 157) < *ḥaṣara*, 'to get caught'.

Khaḍram, 'to become green' < *khaḍḍar*, dissim. *-dd-* > *-dr-*, or < *akhḍar*, 'green'.

Khardam, *khaghdam*, 'to cause s.o. to bleed as a result of dropping him/her to the ground', (Gīl, 80; YD, *Sefat*, 166).

Qarçam, *qaghçam*, 'to cut from the end', 'to nibble', *garḍam*, CA, 'same', (Bak, 380).

Talgham, 'to cause damage', (Gīl, 156); 'to complicate matters', (YD, *Sefat*, 164).

B. 3.2. Type 1 2.3. N

The final radical *n* originated historically as a suffixed morpheme. Most quadriliteral verbs of this type in CA and Arabic dialects originated from nouns that end with *n*, namely, from *'asmā' al-ma'nā*, and Aramaic nouns terminating with *nā*. Indeed, the suffix *n* in combination with certain vowels has proved to be a productive element in the formation of Arabic (and Hebrew) nouns and adjectives.

---

70 See examples of the morphemes M. N. R. T. and 'Ain added to trilateral or doubled verbs in CA: Ṭobī, 75–6, Kāmil, 18, 53–8; al-Suyūṭī, *al-Muzhir*, II, 256–60.

Several quadriliteral verbs 1. 2. 3. N in IA are a result of dissimilation, borrowing, and suffixing. Examples in IA include[71] the following:

'Aswan, 'to become difficult, hard', 'to become stubborn' < √ *'ṢY*, CA, *y* > *w*, (Sām, 171).

'Aqlan, 'to rationalize' < *'aql*, 'intellect', *'aqlānī*, 'rational', (EB, 753).

Baṭlan, 'to get tired', (Ḥajj, *al-Amthāl*, 232, n. 25).

Dashman, 'to upholster' < Per, *dōshama*, 'upholstery', (Wood, 170).

Dastan, 'to plan in advance carefully and orderly', (Bak, 218), Per, *dasteh*, 'order'.

Dharban, 'to be dirty' < *dhirb*, 'dirt', (Sām, 162; MM, 302; Ḥana, *Mu'jam*, III, 135), or 'to be full of *dhubbān* (flies)' < *dhabbān*, dissim. *-bb-* > *-rb-* (the *r* is an infix), 'to fake weakness and inability', (Sām, 162).

Farshan, 'to have the intellectual ability to distinguish among things', Syr, *furshānā*, 'maturity and reasoning', (FM, 417).

Farṭan, ('Awwād, 24); 'to be angry', (Sām, 173; Baz, 124) < *farṭanah*, 'turmoil', (al-Karmilī, *Majmū'ah*, II, 284, n. 9), a term used by sailors and seamen for the heaving sea (Bak, 360), Syr, *fṭan*, 'to make noise, chaos', (FM, 414), *tfarṭan*, 'to behave inappropriately', (Sām, 173); 'to evacuate the bowels' (infant), (Bak, 360).

Farzan, 'to distinguish', 'to see clearly', (Wood, 349); 'to set apart', (Thin, 110; Sām, 173, 'to separate); 'to decipher', as in *farzan il-khaṭṭ*, 'he deciphered the letter', (Ḥana, *Mu'jam*, II, 506), *tfarzan*, 'to be educated' < Per, *fārzanah*, 'a wise person', 'intelligence', (Stein, 918[72]; Shīr, 118, 'to become a queen', Per, *farzīn*, 'queen'; < *faraza*, 'to sort'+suffix *n*, [Sam 173; Thin, 110]).

Ḥalfan, *tḥalfan*, 'to exchange', Arm, *mékhalōpéh*, (YM I, *Hebrew-Aramaic*, 257), or 'to become an alliance, companion' < *ḥalīf*, 'friend, companion', CA.

Harkal, 'to become old, weak', (DH, *Qāmūs*, 292).

Héman, 'to loaf aimlessly', (al-Karmilī, *Majmū'ah*, II, 304, n. 28) < *hāma*, CA, 'same'.

Jaghban, 'to become solid and hard after being fresh and soft' < Syr, *ghbān*, or dissim. of *jabbana*.

Jarban, 'to claim to know it all, contrary to the fact', (Sām, 155).

Khalgan, 'to become worn out and dirty' (clothes), (Ḥajj, *al-Amthāl*, IV, 135), *khaliq*, 'shabby', CA.

Khalṭan, 'to mix' < *khalaṭa*, CA, 'same', (Wood, 132).

---

71 For more examples of *n* pheme suffixed to triliteral verbs in CA, see al-Suyūṭī, *al-Muzhar*, cited in Sām, 53, 54; in other dialects, see Kāmil, 17–18, 53–4, Ṭobī,, 75.

72 F. Steingass, *Comprehensive Persian-English Dictionary* (New Delhi 1996), (henceforth Stein).

Khargal, hargal, 'to shake' (dice), 'to shuffle' (cards), (Gīl, 76; Cha, *Kalimāt*, 72; Thin 281; YD; 151).

Laṭman, 'to slap, strike the face with the hand' < *laṭama*, CA, 'same'.

Makhṭan, makhaṭa, CA, 'to blow the nose', (Sām, 181) , 'to become like *mukhāṭ* (mucus)'.

Raftan, 'to shove', 'to drive away' < *raffat*, 'to dismiss', *-ff-* > *-ft-*, Per, 'going', (Ch, *Kalimāt*, 92; Wood, 190).

Rahdan, 'to arrange', *trahdan*, 'to settle well', (Sām, 163).

Rahwan, 'to amble' (horse), CA, (DH, *Qāmūs*, 125); 'to walk easily and quickly', Per, *rāh*, 'way', *wān*, 'adequate [to travel]', (Cha, *Kalimāt*, 94).

Wahdan, 'to mislead', 'to lead astray', (Wood, 504; Bak, 496; Sām, 183; Ḥana, *Mu'jam*, II, 139).

B. 3.3. Type 1.2.3. L

The *l* as a suffix on triliteral verbs is found in Aramaic, Syriac, Arabic dialects and in the Soqotri dialect in Ethiopia, (Kāmil, 16, 50). Examples from IA:

Darqal, 'to go quickly' (person), 'to hurry up', CA; 'to run into an obstacle', 'to trip over'; Arm, *médarqōléh*; 'same'; 'to roll down' (ball, stone), (YM I, *Hebrew-Aramaic*, 230); Tur, *dakralmak* < 'same'.

Marghal, < *maragha*, 'to roll in dust or mud', (Mac, I, 416) < CA, *tamarragha*, 'same'. It I seen in the expressions *mitmarghal ibdamm il-miçātīl*, (lit. 'he rolls in the blood of the killed'), or *mitmalṭikh ibdamm el-miçātīl*, 'stained by the blood of those killed', said about s.o. who boasts about s.th. he did not do (Turj, 99).

Qaḥṭal and *gaṭṭal*, 'to acquire a different colour due to exposure to the sun or washing s.th. in water' < *qaḥḥala*, dissim. - *ḥḥ* - > *-ḥt-* (Bak, 382), more commonly *tqaḥṭal*, 'to be contracted and have spasms' (in the leg), (Sām, 176).

Qarzal, 'to collect randomly', (Thin, 140; MM, 262). In CA, 'to coif a woman's hair', 'to beautify' < *qaraza*, 'to curl', 'to form a ball', 'to thicken'. This verb is attested in Hebrew, *qirzél*, tr., 'to curl'.

Pashkal, bashkal, 'to twist s.th. and tie it', (Ḥana, *Mu'jam*, I, 695), 'to wobble when walking' < Syr. *fashkil*, 'to rise a lot', (dough), *tfashkal*, 'to do s.th. carelessly', Arm, *ithpashkal*, 'to stumble', (Cha, *Ath*, 26); 'to be in a mess', 'to be confused', (Bak, 468), *mfashkal* < *fuskul*, 'one who has weak hands or legs', said usually about a horse that finishes a race last, (Cha, *Kalimāt*, 184).

Zédal, 'to add', 'to increase', 'to become like Zayd', (Kāmil, 17).

B. 3.4. Type 1.2.3. Sh

Examples:

'Anqash, 'to hang s.th. on a nail', (Bak, 346), CA, *'aniqa*, 'to hold the neck of an animal and hang on it', (*Muḥīṭ*, 639).

'Arbash, 'to branch out and intertwine' (tree), (Sām, 171), 'to print plants and branches on fabric', Heb, *'aréb*, 'a mixture', (Gīl, 248).

Fardash, 'to divide' (food); 'to scatter' <*farrada*, (Thin, 110).

Harbash, 'to become old', (Shāl, III, 151; Dabb, 95; Sām, 183); 'to speak nonsense through anxiety'; (Thin, 279; Ḥajj, *al-Amthāl*, 155, n. 56), *mharbash*, 'old confused person', (Sām, 183).

Ḥakrash < *ḥarkatha*, CA, 'to move s.th.', (*th* > *sh*), *tḥakrash*, 'to move a little' (intr.) (Sām, 157). However, it is possible that the *r* is an infix, as in *ḥakasha al-nār,* CA, 'he moved the burning pieces of wood' (in order to keep the flames burning), and figuratively, 'to incite', (DH, *Qāmūs*, 87), 'to stir, move' (tr.), (Ghanīmah, 271).

Kahwash, *gahwash*, 'to look for s.th. and take it', (Sām, 179).

Kambash, 'to stoop', 'to hunker down', (Ḥajj, *al-Amthāl*, 222).

Kharṭash, 'to cut a few leaves from a tree', (Sām, 159) < *kharaṭa*, 'to remove'.

Nagrash, *naqrash*, ('Awwād, 25), 'to peck a little', *naqara*, 'same', (Gīl, 259; YD, *Sefat*, 272).

Naghbash, 'to cause a tickling sensation', (Bak, 482).

Nakhbash, 'to poke around', 'to rummage a little', 'to look for s.th.', (Bak, 482); 'to dig a hole', (Gīl, 259; 'Ubaydī, 50); 'to uncover the faults of others', fig., (Mac, I, 416) < *nakhaba*, 'to dig', (Sām, 182).

Qarmash, and *qarmaç*, ('Awwād, 24), 'to nibble', 'to cut from the edges of s.th', (Thin, 126; Bak, 393); 'to eat s.th. dry which makes a sound', (Wehr, 759).

Ragṭash, *raqṭash*, < *raqqasha*, 'to decorate by making a few small dots' (on leather or fabric), dissim. *qq* > *qt*, (Sām, 163).

B. 3.5. Type 1.2.3. S

Examples:

Fargaṣ, 'to swell' (skin) and have blisters', 'to become inflamed' < *faqqaṣa*, dissim. -*qq*- > -*rq*-, (Sām, 173; Wood, 351) , *tfargaṣ*, 'to become blistered', (Mac, I, 436). The metaphoric expression, *fargaṣ galbī*, IA, means 'he caused me pain and made me tired', (lit. 'he caused blisters in my heart'), (Thin, 111); 'to breach an agreement', or 'to fall through' < *fugaṣ*, (Wood, 358). The *r* is an infix.

Ḥagraṣ, 'to sit restlessly as if bothered by an insect < *ḥurqūṣ*, 'a type of worm', then the radical *r* exchanged places with g (metathesis) , or < *qaraṣa*, 'to pinch' and the *ḥ* is a prefix, 'to move from one's seat', (Sām, 157), 'to shiver', 'to have an orgasm' (vulg.), (Ḥana, *Mu'jam*, II, 421); 'to pen', 'to hurt', CA, 'to fry meat' where *s* > *ṣ*. (DH, *Qāmūs*, 87). The expression *tḥargiṣ tmargis* is 'she is moving and dancing', (Dul, 37). *Qalfas*, 'to stink', (Ḥajj, *al-Amthāl*, 55, n. 55), *mqalfas*, (epithet), 'untidy', 'short', (Sām, 177).

B. 3.6. Type 1.2.3. '

The ' suffix on triliteral verbs exists mainly in some Yemenite and North African dialects (Kāmil, 18). In CA we find it in *farza'a* < *faraza*, 'to separate', *darqa'a* < *daraqa*, and *karṭa'a*, < *kariṭa*, (Kāmil, 18); in IA, *ṭarga'* is 'to beat' (eggs); 'to clatter', (Wood, 289); 'to burn' (children's speech in Basra, Dul, 149) < Arm, *ṭargha'*, 'turmoil', *mṭarga'*, 'cracked', 'slack' (voice), (Mac, II, 516).

Zagrad, 'to sing', 'to twitter'. ('Awwād 23) < *garrada*, 'same'.

B. 3.7. Type 1.2.3. R

The consonant *r* as a suffix morpheme of quadriliteral verbs exists mainly in Amharic and Tijrani. In IA, I found only *za'bar 'alā*, 'to cheat', (DH, *Qāmūs*, 131; Wehr, 376); 'to talk nonsense' (Gīl, 104); *mza'bir*, 'one who practices jugglery', (DH, *Qāmūs*, 263) < *zabara*. The ' is an infix.

Nagbagh, *negbar*, ('Awwād, 25) 'to fetch', 'to dig', (Gīl, 266; Ben-Jacob, *Hebrew and Aramaic*, 150; YD, *Sefat*, 257; Thin, 251; 'to make holes', Mac, I, 416); Arm, *ménaqbōréh*, (YM I, *Hebrew-Aramaic*, 270) < *naqara*, 'same'.

Ja'far, ('Awwād, 23), 'to cut' (tree) < *ja'afa*, 'same', or *ju'iltu fidāk* (CA, 'May I be your ransom'), (*Muḥīṭ*, 112).

B. 3.8. Type 1.2.3. B.

The consonant *b* as a suffixed morpheme on triliteral verbs is rare in Semitic languages. There are only a few examples in CA: *zaldaba* < *zalada, zaghdaba* < *zaghada*. In IA, I found only the verb *daḥlab* in a children's folk song (Q, I:439; Masliyah, 'The Folk Songs of Iraqi Children', *JSS* 55:2 [2010], 560, Song 14: *Bam Bam Bam!*; Bak, 226) < *dalbaḥa* < *dalaḥa*, CA, 'same', 'to bend one's back because of carrying a heavy load', (metathesis), (Ḥana, *Mu'jam*, III, 77; Sām, 160). In the Kuwaiti dialect, this verb means the 'same', (Ḥana, *al-Alfāẓ*, 128). However, it is most likely that the infix *l* is added after the second radical of the triliteral verb *ḥadiba*, 'to bend', (*Muḥīṭ*, 152), i.e. *ḥadiba* > *ḥadlaba* > *daḥlaba*. Another possibility is that the *b* is suffixed to the verb *daḥala*, CA, 'to dig the sides of a well', 'to conceal o.s.'.

Haftar, ('Awwād, 23), 'to peel'.

B. 39. Type 1.2.3. t or ṭ (but some are not suffixes)

A few of the following verbs are also classified above in different categories.

Barqaṭ, 'to shine' < *baraqa*, CA.
Gashmaṭ, ('Awwād, 24), 'to scrape off', CA, *qashaṭa*, 'same'.
Kashmaṭ, see *ghashmaṭ*.
Laghmaṭ, 'to sully', 'to smear', (Thin, 192); 'to cover up', (Wood, 423).
Sharbaṭ', 'to fill gaps with cement and water', (Bak, 285), 'to put on watery cement', 'to do s.th. quickly and carelessly', (Mac, I, 416).
Sha'faṭ, ('Awwād, 24), 'to drink s.th. in one gulp' < *sha'afa*, CA, 'same'.
Zaghlaṭ, 'to deceive', 'to make a mistake in accounts purposely', (Ḥana, *Mu'jam*, III, 249; Mac, I, 416; Shāl, III, 355; Sām, 164), *zaghila*, 'to cheat'.

C. 3. Deriving Quadriliteral Verbs by Procedures other than by A or B above: 1. Denominatives, 2. Composition and Blends

C. 3.1. Denominatives

In CA, we find quadriliteral verbs that are derived from proper and common nouns, like *athama*, 'to travel to Tihāmah'; *a'raqa*, 'to go to Iraq'; *ash'ama*, 'to enter Damascus'; *'aṣhara*, 'to go to the desert; *'anjada*, 'to go to Najd', *ajnaba*, 'to go southward'; *aṣbaḥa*, 'to get up in the morning' < *ṣabāḥ*, 'morning', *aḍla'a*, 'to limp' < *ḍil'*, 'a limp'; *narjasa*, 'to put *nirjis'*, Per, *narges* (narcissus)'. Likewise, there exists a considerable number of quadriliteral verbs in IA that are derived from Arabic common nouns and non-Arabic denominatives.

Examples:

'Ab'ab, 'to stuff one's pocket', (Mac, 418, 427) < *'ubb*, 'a pocket or fold in the breast of the folding gown', (Sām, 199).

'Aç'aç, 'to become fat like a *'ikkah*' (a skin container for storing fat), (Shāl, II, 358).

'Afrat < 'to become an *'ifrīt*' (a demon), (Sām, 190; Ḥana, *Mu'jam*, II, 78; Shāl, III, 237).

'Aj'aj, 'to stir up dust' < *'ajāj*, 'dust', (Wood, 302; Thin 82, n. 11), 'to roar'.

'Ak'ak, 'to become fat' < *'ikk*, 'fat', (Thin, 94, n. 64).

'Al'al, 'to make s.o. sick' < *'alīl*, 'sick', 'weak', (Gīl, 173; Sām, 198), *m'al'al*, 'shaky', 'out of order', (YD, *Sefat*, 247); Arm, *mé'alōléh*, 'to suffer', (YM I, *Hebrew-Aramaic*, 333) or 'to browse' (pages), (YD, *Sefat*, 247; YM I, *Hebrew-Aramaic*, 358).

'Anwan, 'to write an address' < *'inwān* 'address', (Erwin, *A Short Reference*, 78).

'Aṣ'aṣ, 'to get stuck' (key) √ 'ṢY, 'to be stubborn', 'to complicate matters', (Bak, 338), 'to become hard, firm', (Cha, *Ath*, 66), Arm, *'aṣ'ūṣ*, 'tailbone'. The Iraqi folk poet uses this verb to indicate an unchanged situation, *gabul rizqak 'aṣ'aṣ* (*qūt ibqūtah wu-mkhaṣṣaṣ, il-yōm mqarnaṣ mrayyash*), 'in the past your livelihood was the same, (in each meal, a cut and featherless *lhémī* bird, but today the bird has a lots of feathers and it soars)', (Shāl, III, 380).

'Ash'ash, 'to build a nest' < *'ishsh*, 'nest'.

'Ashwash, 'to be dim-sighted', (DH, *Qāmūs*, 194).

'Ath'ath, 'to be worm-eaten'< *'ithth*, 'worms'; 'to spread and scatter', (Thin, 81).

'Az'az, *t'az'az*, 'to act hard to get', (Bak, 123), *'izz*, 'glory'; 'to have sex', < *'azza*, (slang, Jews in Baghdad), (YD, *Sefat*, 216).

Baghdad, 'to travel to Baghdad', 'to adopt the customs of Baghdadis', (Kāmil, 65), *tbaghdad*, 'to behave like a Baghdadi' (Mac, I, 436).

Aqlam, 'to acclimatize', (EB, 763) < *'iqlim*, 'climate'.

'Awlam, 'to globalize', (EB, 763), *'ālam*, 'world'.

Bakhnaq/g, *tbakhnag*, 'to veil' < *bukhnuq*, 'veil'.

Bal'am, ('Awwād, 22), 'to swallow greedily' < *bala'a*, CA, 'to swallow' < *bal'ūm*, 'throat', (Sām, 154); 'to astound', 'to dumbfound', (Wood, 42), *tbal'am*, 'to be unable to speak', (Bak, 112), 'to be gulped', (Mac, 436); 'to stutter', (Ḥana, *Mu'jam*, II, 25).

Balsām, 'to become sad' < *mublis*, CA, 'sad', (Sām, 139).

Bardag, 'to cause pain and suffering' < Per, *bardāg*, 'pain', (Baz, 23; MM, 63; Shāl, I, 321).

Bardak, 'to recount legends', Per. *bardak*, (Cha, *Kalimāt*, 16).

Barqa', *barga'*, 'to put on a veil' < *burqu'*, 'a veil', CA, (Sām, 153; Ḥana, *Mu'jam*, II, 502), *tbarga'*, 'to cover one's face'.

Barṭal, ('Awwād, 22), 'to bribe' < *barṭil* , Per, 'same', (Sām, 153; Ḥana, *Mu'jam*, I, 496; Mac, 421).

Barṭam, 'to pout', 'to be angry', (Mac I, 420; Bak, 76; Sām, 153) < *burṭūm*, IA, 'thick lips', (Ḥana, *Mu'jam*, I, 497).

Basmar, *masmar*, 'to nail', (Wood, 35; Sām, 54, 425; DH, *Qāmūs*, 265), < *mismār* and *busmār*, CA, *bézméra*, 'nail', *tbasmar*, 'to be nailed', (Ḥana, *Mu'jam*, I, 524; Mac, I, 433).

Ça'ça', 'to shape s.th. (usually fabric) like a doughnut and put it on the head in order to carry a load', (Ḥana, *Mu'jam*, II, 293).

Çangal, 'to hang on a hook', (Gīl, 147; Sām, 156; TA, 42; YD, *Sefat*, 195) < Tur, *çengel*, Per, *çangāl*, Arm, *çéngalah*, 'fork', 'hook', (YM I, *Hebrew-Aramaic*, 125).

Çarçab, 'to frame', (Mac, I, 421; Wood, 84) < OTur, *çarçube*, (var. of Tur, *çerçeve*), Per, *çahār*, 'four'+ *çub*, 'piece of wood', (Turj, 37; Ḥana, *Mu'jam*, I, 689; MM, 126).

Danbas and *dambas*, 'to pin', 'to clip' < *danbūs* and *dambūs* < *dabbūs*, 'a pin', (Sām, 162; Gīl, 92; Wood, 164; Ḥana, *Mu'jam*, III, 86; YD, *Sefat*, 143). This quadriliteral verb is formed from the dissemination of *dabbūs* > *danbūs*, (*bb*<*nb*).

Darham, ('Awwād, 23), 'to have a lot of money', *dirham*, 'dirham', 'money'.

Darwash, 'to have unkempt hair like a dervish', (Gīl, 89), or 'to live like a dervish', Per, *dar*, 'door' and *vīsh* , 'carpet', 'a piece of fabric', 'one who lies in the front of the house', < *darpīsh*, Per, 'an epithet for a begger', (Baz, 76; Shīr, 62).

Dashman, 'to upholster'< *dōshama*, Per, 'upholstering', (Wood, 170).

Dédā, 'to sing a *didiyyah'* (lullaby), (Bak, 231), 'swing', (Sām, *al-Tawzī'*, 135[73]).

Danfash, 'to fluff up or out' (hair, feathers) < *nafasha*, 'same'.

Dhōban, 'to be full of flies and dirt', (Qad, II, 121; Ḥana, *Mu'jam*, III, 140).

Far'an, *tfar'an*, 'to become a *far'ūn*' (pharaoh), i.e. 'a tyrant', (Ḥana, *Mu'jam*, II, 84; Sām, 190; Shāl, III, 44).

Farhad, 'to loot', (Sām, 174; Mac, I, 425) <*fahada*, 'to be strong and active', (Shīr, 119). The *r* is an infix. The origin of this verb is unknown, but it is likely that it came from *farhūd*, CA, 'a cub', 'a proper name denoting a courageous and strong person', who apparently led the mob attack against the Jews of Baghdad in June 1941 following Nazi propaganda in Iraq and the rise of pro-Nazi elements there.

Gamark, 'to pay customs on imported goods' < *gumruk*, Tur, 'customs'.

Haylam, *hélam*, ('Awwād, 25), 'to wander aimlessly'; 'to go around with no purpose or job', (YD, *Sefat*, 125; Gīl, 274, Shīr, 57); 'to work with ambition', (Bak, 508).

Ḥazqal, *Ḥasqal* < CA, 'to economize', (Ben-Jacob, *Hebrew and Aramaic*, 64), 'to save money', 'to buy items cheaply', (MM, 141; Sām, 157; Ḥana, *Mu'jam*, II, 365; Mac, I, 421). It is derived from a Jewish name, *Hisqél* or 'Ezekiel', (Ben-Jacob, *Hebrew and Aramaic*, 166), who is to some Iraqis a symbol of thriftiness and tightfistedness. However, in Hebrew, the verb *ḥasakh* means 'to save', (money), indicating that the *l* in *ḥasqal* is a suffix.

Ḥéwan, 'to make s.o. act like an animal', *tḥewan*, 'to behave like an animal' (*ḥayawān*) 'animal', 'to do s.th. stupid', (Bak, 115; Gīl, 35).

Kabrat , 'to coat with *kibrīt*' (sulphur).

Kharbaṭ, Syr, *ḥbaṭ*, less commonly *khalbaṭ*, 'to throw into disorder, 'to disarrange'.

Karkam, 'to become yellow', 'to add turmeric', *tkarkam*, 'to become pale', (Plamenta, II, 429); *mékarkōméh*, 'same', (YM II, *Aramaic-Kurdish*, 260) < *kurkum*, 'turmeric', Arm, *karkimā*, 'a saffron plant'.

Karshan, 'to acquire a *kirsh*' (a pot-belly), (Wood, 402).

Kazbar, ('Awwād, 23), 'to shiver'; 'to feel a weird sensation', (Thin, 142; Sām, 191).

73 Ibrāhīm al-Sāmurrā'ī, *al-Tawzī' al-Lughawī al-Jughrāfī fī al-'Irāq* (Baghdad 1968), (henceforth Sām, *al-Tawzī'*).

Khandaq, (ʿAwwad, 23), 'to dig a trench' < *khandaq*, 'a trench' < Per, *kandéh* (AN, 183[74]).

Ḥanfash and *ḥamfash*, 'to be enraged; (Bak, 181); 'to have unkempt hair or feathers', (Mac, I, 216) < *ḥanfish*, ʿa dog with thick hair', (Ḥana, *Mu'jam*, II, 420; Qad, II, 121; Wood, 403).

Khastak, 'to become sick'; (Bak, 191) < *khastéh*, Per, OTur, 'sick', 'wounded', 'to demolish s.th. and make it unworkable'. *kōsaj*, *tkōsaj*, 'to become crazy', because he has a long beard, < Per, *kōsah*, '(a man) with a small beard'.

Kōzal, *kōzar*, 'to separate hay unsuitable for feeding from grains', 'to have lumps of s.th. remaining in the sieve after polishing rice or wheat' < Arm, *gāwzālā*, (Cha, *Ath*, 78).

La'la', 'to glow'< *lu'lu'a*, 'pearl', CA.

Madhhab, *tmadhhab*, 'to follow a sect, a creed' < *madhhab*, 'creed'; *mitmadhhib*, 'being improvished and miserable', (Ḥana, *Mu'jam*, III, 141).

Maḍḥak, *tmaḍḥak*, 'to mock', (Altoma, 59).

Maḍraṭ, more commonly *tmaḍraṭ*, 'to make an ass of o.s.', 'to boast'; 'to pretend to be knowledgeable', (Shāl, III, 324); 'to fabricate', (Wood, 440) < Arm, *zéraṭa*, Tur, *zarṭa*, 'breaking wind'.

Maḥlā, *tmaḥlā*, 'to like', 'to find s.th. sweet', (Bak, 132), *ḥulu*, 'sweet', handsome'.

Mandal, (ʿAwwād, 25), 'to perfume o.s. with *mandal*' (aromatic wood when burnt).

Markaz, *tmarkaz*, 'to become firmly fixed', 'to settle', (Altoma, 59; Mac, I, 436); 'to become concentrated' < *markaz*, 'centre'.

Ma'mak, (ʿAwwād, 25), *ma'aka*, CA, 'to scrub clothes', (Bak, 466), Heb, *ma'akh*, 'to crush, squash'; 'to knead', (YD, *Sefat*, 43).

Masṭar, 'to show a sample', Arm, *masṭara*, 'a ruler', Ita, *mosṭra*, 'sample'; 'to make stand in single file', (TA, 170); 'to draw a straight line', (Wood, 440). This verb is attested in the Kuwaiti dialect and the other Gulf counties, (Ḥana, *al-Alfāẓ*, 204; Qaf, 381[75]).

Méḥan, 'to confuse' < *miḥnah*, CA, 'confusion', (Bak, 55).

Méjan, 'to sing a *mejānāh*' (a type of Arabic folk song) < *nagham*, 'melody'.

---

74 ʿAlī Nūr-al-Dīn, *al-Ta'rīb wa-'Āthāruhu fī al-'Arabiyyah wal-Fārisiyyah* (Cairo 1979), (henceforth AN).

75 Hamdi Qafisheh, *Gulf Arabic-English Dictionary* (Chicago 1997) (henceforth Qaf).

Nésan, (ʻAwwād, 25), ʻto approach, the month of Nīsān' (April), in Yemen (Piamenta, II, 502). The verb is used as an agricultural term denoting a certain constellation of stars which herald an appropriate time to plant seeds'.

Paçwar, ʻto speak nonsense or foul language', (fig., Ḥana, *Mu'jam*, I, 30) < Tur, *paçavra*, ʻrag', (Cha, *Kalimāt*, 29).

Qarban, ʻto make fall i a trap', (Gīl, 212), ʻto hit hard', (YD, *Sefat*, 176) < *qurbān*, sacrifice'.

Qandal, ʻto glow', ʻto glare like a *qindīl*', (Sām, 190; Bak, 396; Thin, 133; Wood, 379), ʻto light a *qindīl*' < *candela*, (Lat.), Arm, *qandélah*, (YM II, *Aramaic-Kurdish*, 370), *tqandal*, ʻto be intoxicated', (Bak, 396). *dīl* is an oil amp consisting of a glass bowl filled to two-thirds of its capacity with oil in which a wick is partially immersed.

Ṣandaq, ʻto put items in a chest' < Per *ṣandūq*, ʻa box', ʻa case', (Shīr, 108).

Ṣangar, ʻto stand like the eagle', (IA, *ṣigar*), ʻeagle', (Sām, 190).

Sarsam, *tsarsam*, ʻto lose consciousness because of a high fever' < *sarsām*, Per, ʻheadache', *sar*, ʻhead', *sam*, ʻpain', ʻpoison', (TA, 35; Cha, *Kalimāt*, 111).

Shakban, ʻto fill a *shukbān*', Per, ʻsack containing goods', (Sām, 189).

Sharnaq, ʻto sparkle' < *sharqūtah*, ʻa spark'.

Shōlab, ʻto sieve' < *shālūbī*, ʻa small sieve', (Bak, 281).

Ṭarkham, < *tarkham*, *t* > *ṭ* and √ RKM > √ RKhM), ʻto be filled with mucus' (chest), (Sām, 170).

Tarmakh < *ṭarkhan*, ʻto be absent-minded', ʻto feel sleepy after eating', *ṭarkhinah'*, (Per. *ṭarkhineh*), ʻa dish made with sour milk and cooked bulgar wheat believed to cause drowsiness', (Bak, 321), *mṭarkhan/m*, ʻsleepy', (Cha, *Ath*, 83).

Tarmas, (ʻAwwād, 24), ʻto be dumb, stupid', ʻto be absent', CA, *tarmas* > *tarmās*, ʻstupid', (Cha, *Kalimāt*, 36).

Tarya', ʻto burp', (Wood, 56) < *taryū'ah*, ʻa burp'.

Za'ṭaṭ, *ṭza'ṭaṭ*, ʻto behave childishly', *za'ṭūṭ*, ʻsmall child', (Erwin, *A Short Reference*, 80).

Zahlaj/g, ʻto make slip', (Mac, I, 416); ʻto become yellow mostly due to anaemia', (Bak, 255); ʻto become sticky and smelly', (Sām, 164; Gīl, 106; YD, *Sefat*, 37).

Taznan, ʻto act like a *zan*' (Per, ʻwoman'), (Cha, *Kalimāt*, 40).

Zakrat, *tzakrat*, ʻto dress nicely like a bachelor'. This verb is attested also in the Kuwaiti dialect, (Ḥana, *al-Alfāẓ*, 161) < Tur, *zugurt*, ʻpenniless', (Thin, 48; Ḥana, *al-Alfāẓ*, 161), Tur, *zugurti*.

Zangan, ʻto bestow wealth', (Wood, 207; Cha, *Kalimāt*, 52) < Tur, *zengin*, ʻrich', (MM, 178).

Zangaṭ, ʻto have pimples' < Syr, *zezanṭa*, IA, *zunguṭah* (MM, 179; Wood, 207).

Zōmal, *tzémal*, 'to act stupidly like a donkey', *zmāl*, IA, 'donkey', (Erwin, *A Short Reference*, 800).

*C. 3.2. Quadriradical Verbs Resulting from Composition (***Naḥt***) and Blends*

Included in this type are quadriliteral verbs which are formed by combing two words with suppression of a part of each. The resulting form suggests something of the meaning of each blended word. In blending two verbs, it occurs rarely that both verbs have the same or close meaning to each other.

There are many examples of Arabic compound quadriradical lexical items in medieval literature and modern technical dictionaries. These are formed by attaching parts of two verbs or a verb and a noun, or by contracting frequent expressions. As far as quadriliteral verbs are concerned, there are no rules in forming them except that they should conform with Arabic patterns and phonology. Several of these are contractions and others are denominatives, compositions and blends of two verbs, or borrowed from other languages.

Basmal, 'to invoke God's name', (*ism Allāh*), CA, (Mac, I, 421).

'Abwal, 'to think' < *'ala+bāl*, (lit. 'it came to mind').

Baḥṣaṣ, CA, *ḥaṣaba*, 'to pave with small pebbles'.

Ba'thar, 'to scatter' = *baḥatha*, 'to find out'+ *badhara*, 'to sow', 'to scatter', (Sām, 139).

Bahdal, *bahdhal* = *badhala+bahala*, (Sām, 154), or *badhdhala*, dissim. > dhdh > *hdh*; Arm, *bhatthā*, 'shame', (Cha, *Ath*, 23); 'to insult', ('Ubaydī, 48).

Barkash, 'to cause trouble', (Ḥana, *Mu'jam*, I, 501), *tbarkash*, 'to stick to the clothes', (e.g. thorns, ants, wasps) < Per, *bar*, 'load'+*kash*, 'carrier', (Baz, 24); 'to cheat' < *barkas*, (*s* > *sh*), (Sām, 153).

Çarqa' = composition of two verbs, *çarqa'+qarqa'*, which means the 'same', 'to become torn, worn out and noisy', (Gīl, 248).

Dam'aza = *adāma allāhu 'izzaka* (CA, 'May God prolong your glory').

Ḥamdala = 'to say, *al-ḥamdu lillāh*' (CA, 'praise be God').

Ḥasbal, *ḥazbal* = (*ḥasab+bāl*, 'in the opinion of s.o.', as in *inṭéthā flūs ḥazbālī 'ādmī*, 'I gave him money; I thought he was honorable man', (Wood, 102).

Darbaz, 'to lock the door from the inside', (*Muḥīṭ*, 274), but in Persian it means 'opened door', *dar*, 'door'+ *bāz*, 'opened'; *daraza* 'to sew closely' (dress). The *b* is an infix, (*Muḥīṭ*, 276).

Dahwar, 'to hurl down' = *dāra*, 'to turn'+*hadara*, 'to push'.

Farfak, 'to rub a lot' = *dalaka*, 'to massage'+*faraka*, 'to rub', or <*faraka*, CA, 'to rub', (Wehr, 710). This verb is attested also in the Lebanese dialect (AF, *Mu'jam*, 128).

Farkath, 'to separate' <*faraka*, 'to rub'+*faratha*, 'to cut and scatter', (Thin, 111; Sām, 174).

Farqaṭ, *fargaṭ*, 'to cut s.th. into small pieces, CA, <*farraqa*, 'to separate'+ *raqqaṭa*, 'to add spots' (garment), (Sām, 163) <*farkath*, 'same'.

Qarṭaf, 'to cut a small piece of hair', 'to pluck feathers' = *qaraṭa*, 'to cut'+*qaṭafa*, 'to pick a flower, a fruit', (Sām, 175; Dul, 15); 'to trim, clip', (Wood, 387), *mgarṭaf*, an epithet for a weak, mentally disabled person', (Shāl, II, 121).

Ḥawqala = 'to say *lā ḥawla walā quwwatan illā billāh*' (CA, 'there is no power and strength save in God'), *ḥōqal*, 'same'; (Mac, 416), *ḥōqal 'alā*, 'to watch s.o.', (DH, *Qāmūs*, 92; Ḥana, *al- Alfāẓ*, 103).

Ḥay'ala = *ḥayyun 'alā al-ṣalāt, ḥayyun 'alā al-falāh*, CA, an expression calling worshippers 'to come to prayer'.

Haylala = *la ilāha illā allāh* (CA, 'there is no God but Allah').

Hélal, [to say] *la ilāha illā Allāh* (CA, 'there is no God but Allah').

Ja'fada = *ju'iltu fidāka* (CA, 'May I be your ransom').

Khalbaṭ, 'to mix up' < *khalaṭa*, 'to mix'+*khabaṭa*, 'to beat', (Sām, 180), or *khalaṭa*, 'to mix up'. The *b* is an infix, and *r* > *l*.

Laghmaṭ, 'to sully'= *laghama*, 'to foam at the mouth' (camel) +*ṭ*, 'to cover', (Sām, 180).

Laghwas = *laghu*, 'to chew'+*liwās*, 'food', 'to make a mess', 'to speak incoherently', (Sām, 180), 'to talk nonsense', (Bak, 447)

Ja'lak = *ju'iltu fidāka* (CA, 'May I be your ransom').

Lakhbaṭ, 'to mess up' < *khalbaṭ* (metathesis), or *khalaṭa*+*khabaṭa* (Sām, 180); *tlakhbaṭ*, 'to be confused', 'to be embarrassed', (Bak, 131).

Marḥaba, 'to say *marḥaban*' ('welcome'), (lit. 'God loves' [you]) < *mār* = Aramaic word used by the first Christians+*ḥbā*, Arm, 'love' (informal).

Mashkana = *mā shā'a allāhu kāna*, 'whatever God wants, will be'.

Qarmash, ('Awwād, 24), 'to eat s.th. dry' = *qarasha*, 'to gnash'+*qarama*, 'to cut'.

Qarmaṭ, *gharmaṭ* = *qarama*, 'to cut down'+*qaraṭa*, 'to nibble'. The *m* is an infix+ *qaraṭa*, 'to nibble'; 'to be thrifty', (Sām, 176; Thin, 126, n. 27); 'to wrinkle', *méqarmōṭéh* (YM II, *Aramaic-Kurdish*, 296), 'to become a Karmathian', (Piamenta, I, 395); 'to demand and get money', (Wood, 371), *tqarmaṭ*, 'to be wrinkled, twisted' (thread), 'to shrink' (skin), Arm, *ithqarmaṭ*, (Cha, *Ath*, 27).

Qarṭam, *qarḍam*, 'to nibble', *qarmaṭ*, 'to cut down', (Wood, 371) < *qaraḍa* + *qaḍama*, 'same'; 'to crunch', (Sām, 175); 'to nip', (AF, *Mu'jam*, 139; DH, *Qāmūs*, 222), 'to trim' (grass), 'to lop off'.

Rasmal, 'to provide capital', *rās+māl'*, 'to neither gain nor lose in buying and selling goods', (Same 162).

Sabḥala = *subḥāna Allāh*, CA, 'to say praised be to God'.

Ṣal'am = *ṣalla allāhu 'alayhi wa sallama*, to say 'May God have mercy on Him'.

Sam'ala = *as-salāmu 'alaykum*, to say 'Peace be upon you'.

Sarbal, a compound of Persian *sar*, 'above'+*bāl*, 'stature', (TA, 34).

Sarkash, 'to be arrogant, stubborn', (Cha, *Kalimāt*, 112) < Per, *sar*, 'head'+*kash* < Per, *kashīdan*, 'pulling'.

Sha'baṭ, 'to tear'= *sha'aṭa*, 'to make a sound when cutting fabric or skin'+ *'abaṭa*, CA, 'to slaughter', (Sām, 167), or *shabaṭa*. The ' is an infix.

Sha'lab, 'to smoke' (lamp, wood), *sha'ala*, 'to kindle'+ *lahiba*, 'to flame' (intr.), 'to smoke'.

Shakhbaṭ, 'to scribble', *khabaṭa*, 'to mix up'+*shakhaṭa*, 'to cross out', (Sām, 166; Bak, 284; Hanẓal, 356).

Shanhaq, *shanhagh* = *nahaqa*, 'to bray'+*shahaqa*, 'same', or < *shanhaja*, 'to sob' *j* > *q*, (Sām, 168; Bak, 122), or < *nahaqa*, (Rabīn, 154), and the *sh* is a prefix, or *shihag*, IA, 'to have hiccups', (Wood, 251).

Sharbak, 'to tie' = *shark*, 'net'+*shabaka*, 'to intertwine', (Sām, 166; al-Karmilī, *Majmū'ah*, II, 174, n. 5); 'to entangle', (Wood, 238); 'to complicate', (Gīl, 125); *tsharbak*, 'to become entangled', 'to be embarrassed, confused', (DH, *Qāmūs*, 6; Ḥana, *Mu'jam*, II, 66), as in *ishtarbakat yadahu*, CA, 'his hands got confused' < *sharbagh*, Syr, 'to have many knots' (a rope), *rbāgh*, Syr (FM, 274).

Ṭalbaq = *aṭāla allāhu baqā'aka*, 'May God prolong your life'.

Ṭarbaq, 'to make an annoying noise'= *ṭaraqa*, 'to knock'+ *ṭabṭaba*, 'to pat', (Sām, 170; Bak, 318).

Ṭarṭash, 'to splash' (the wall of a building) = *ṭashsha*, 'to scatter'+*rashsha*, 'to spray'; (Kāmil, 22); 'to deafen', (Wood, 288), dissim. *ṭarrash*, *-rr-* > *-rṭ-*.

Zaghlaṭ, 'to deceive in accounts, bills', (Wood, 204) = *ghalaṭa*, 'to make a mistake on purpose'+ *zāghal*, 'to cheat', (Sām, 164).

D. Borrowing from other Semitic Languages and Non-Semitic Languages: Persian, Turkish, English, French, Italian and Greek

Loan words comprise a part of the vocabulary of all languages (E. Sapir, *Language*, [New York 1949], 183, n. 1). In some cases the determination of such loan words is especially difficult because there is a possibility that what was thought to be a loan word is actually an original cognate word which happens to occur in one language but is rare in the sister language. There are a considerable number of borrowed Aramaic, Syriac, Hebrew, Turkish and Persian loan words in Arabic, including quadriliteral verbs, some of which became an integral part of the spoken Iraqi dialect in some regions of the country. I have mentioned above several of these verbs, including Hebrew and Aramaic.

The majority of these verbs are derived from denominatives after the nouns were arabized and their usage had become fairly widespread in Iraq. No drastic morphological changes were required and the quadriliteral verbs are pronounced according to the Arabic pattern *af'ala* (CA) or *af'al* (IA). The following are loan lexical items from Turkish, Persian etc.

D. 1.1. Turkish and Persian

'Anqar, 'to burden', 'to trouble', (MM, 215) < OTur, *angārya*, var. of *ankārya*, 'drudgery', 'a heavy object', (Bak, 346; Thin, 97).

'Aṣmal, *t'aṣmal*, 'to adopt the customs of the Ottomans', (Thin, 253) < *'uṣmallī*, 'Ottoman'.

Bahraj, ('Awwād, 22), 'to adorn', *tbahraj*, 'to beautify o. s.' (woman), 'to become bad, invalid'< Per, *banhāreh*, the *n* is dropped and *h* > *j*; 'to threaten', (Piamenta, I, 42).

Bardag, 'to torture' < *bardagī*, Per, 'slavery', (MM, 63), 'pain and suffering', (Sām, *al-Dakhīl*, 23[76]).

Barmaj, 'to plan' < Per, *barnamāj*, *bar*, 'once', 'load'+ *nāmeh*, 'book', 'letter' (TA, 6).

76 Ibrāhīm al-Sāmurrā'ī, *al-Dakhīl fī al-Fārisiyyah wal-'Arabiyyah* (Lebanon 2001), (henceforth Sām, *al-Dakhīl*).

Barwaz and *parwaz*, (ʿAwwād, 22); 'to frame' < Per, *parvāz*, 'a frame', (Cha, *Kalimāt*, 30; Ḥana, *Mu'jam*, I, 689; TA, 10; DH, *Qāmūs*, 40; YD, *Sefat*, 133).

Çabraz, (ʿAwwād, 23), 'to hook' < Per, *çap*, 'left'+ *rast*, 'right'. It is called so because one side of the hook turns to the left and the other to the right, (Cha, *Kalimāt*, 57); 'to become blurred' (vision), Tur, 'crosswise', and by extension 'cross-eyed'.

Çaḥçal, 'to drag o.s. on the ground', (Gīl, 145; Wood, 214), 'to walk very slowly'; Bak, 262; YD, *Sefat*, 122), < *saḥsal*, 'to pull, drag'.

Çarghṭ, *jarghaṭ*, 'to drink, sip' < *jara'a*, CA, 'same'. First, the Persians borrowed the Arabic word *jar'ah*, 'a sip' as *jarghātu*, then the Arabs derived the verb *çarghaṭ* from the Persian, 'to sip, drink', (Cha, *Kalimāt*, 59).

Çarkhal, *çarçar* 'to shake', 'to wash dishes in a vessel with water' < *çarikh*, 'wheel'. The *l* is a suffix, (MM, 127; Gīl, 146; Ḥana, *Mu'jam*, II, 285; YD, *Sefat*, 149; Cha, *Kalimāt*, 57).

Gandar, 'to roll down', 'to revolve', (Cha, *Ath*, 78), Arm, *mégandōré*, (YM II, *Aramaic-Kurdish*, 71; Thin, 178; Gīl, 60), *itgandar*, 'to be rolled', Arm, *ithgandar*, (Cha, *Ath*, 166).

Çarmaq, 'to make a noise when dragging one's feet in worn-out wooden slippers', (MM, 129; Ḥana, *Mu'jam*, II, 288).

Çarçaq, 'to wet' (the ground), Kur, *çarçīq*, 'wet ground', (Ḥana, *Mu'jam*, II, 284).

Darmak, Tur, 'to collect, gather', 'to sully clothes with flour, dust', (Sām, 161; Ḥana, *Mu'jam*, III, 48), 'to stain', 'to spot'; (Wood, 157). In CA, 'to smooth', (opposite meaning).

Darkal, 'to roll a ball on the ground'< Tur, *dakralmak*.

Dōlab, 'to turn around like a *dūlāb*' (Per, 'water-wheel'), (Naqqāsh, *Nzūlah*, 51), 'to say s.th. repeatedly' like a water wheel that turns around continuously, (Bak, 227); 'to cheat' (fig.), (Ḥana, *Mu'jam*, III, 107; Sām, 188); 'to enter secretly', CA, *dalaba* (YD, *Sefat*, 208); 'to change s.o.'s opinion', 'to convince', (Shīr, 65).

Farzal, 'to shoe' (horse) < *parzala*, Arm, (Cha, *Ath*, 54).

Gamrag, 'to impose a duty or customs on imported goods' < Tur, *gumrug*, 'customs', (Sām, 191). The expression *gamragūh* means 'they extorted high customs on merchandise', (Shāl, II, 576).

Gōman, 'to estimate' < *gmān*, Per, 'opinion', 'estimation', (Thin, 176), *khammana*, 'to estimate', CA.

Kalfat, 'to caulk with asphalt', 'to fill the gaps in the ship's deck' (Sām, 180; MM, 269). It has the same meaning in the Gulf countries, (Qaf, 506) < *kafata*, 'same'.

Kandar, *kandagh*, 'to roll from up to down', (Cha, *Ath*, 78; Bak, 367; ʿUbaydī, 54); 'to shape s.th round' < *kandīr*, 'a large tray made of copper' rolled because of its size and heavy weight, *itkandar*, 'to roll o.s.' < Arm *ithgandar* (Cha, *Kalimāt*, 166, and *Ath*, 78).

Janbash, 'to dance and clap'< Tur, *jumbush*, Per, *jonbesh*, 'movement, agitation', (Stein, 373) a distortion of *ḥanbash*, 'to dance, jump, walk, and play', (Ḥana, *Mu'jam*, II, 237), 'to be confused', (Shāl, I, 520).

Haftak, *haftaj*, 'to speak in seven different ways', Per, *haft*, 'seven'+*tak*, 'single', (Bak, 504); 'to abate', 'to die down' < *hifat* (Wood, 481).

Handam, 'to make neat', 'to dress up s.o.', (Wood, 483); 'to array' < Per, *andām*, 'figure', 'stature', (TA, 75; Sām, 192; Gīl, 273; Mac, I, 483; Thin, 289).

Handas, 'to design', 'to sketch', (Wood, 483; Sām, 192) < Per, *handāzeh*, 'an arm used for measurement', (TA, 75; Cha, *Kalimāt*, 188); Arm, *méhandoséh*; 'to engineer'.

Jalwaz, 'to flatter', 'to cheat', (Sām, 155) < Per, *jalvāz*, 'a cheater'; 'to be like a paste', (YD, *Sefat*, 111).

Jambaz and *janbaz*, 'to cheat', 'to talk a lot' < *jān*+*bāzī*, (Per, lit. 'one who plays with souls'), (Ḥana, *Mu'jam*, II, 236; *al-Alfāẓ*, 319) < *çenebaz*, 'chatty'. In the language of those who breed birds *janbāzī* is 'a broker', a 'cheater', (Thin, 55; Ḥana, *al-Alfāẓ*, 17), *tjanbaz*, 'to be tidy', (MM, 100; Ḥana, *Mu'jam*, II, 34).

Jandar, see *gandar*, (*g* > *j*), 'to roll down' (tr.), (Ghanīmah, 268) < Per, *jandarah*, 'crush', (Stein, 374; Shīr, 5). (YM I, *Hebrew-Aramaic*, 231). *Jarbaz*, 'to deceive', (Shāl, I, 494; Bak, 142; Baz, 53), Per, *gurbuz*, 'a sly person', 'talkative', 'smooth-tongued'.

Kahrab, 'to electrify', Per, (lit. 'to attract straw'), (Thin, 155; Cha, *Kalimāt*, 169; Sām, 187; TA, 65; Thin, 155), Arm, *mékahrōbéh*, (YM I, *Hebrew-Aramaic*, 253).

Kalbaç and *kalbaj*, 'to handcuff', Tur, *kelpeçe*, 'handcuff', (Sām, 191; Kāmil, 22, Ḥana, V, 150), Arm, *mékalbōcé*, (YM I, *Hebrew-Aramaic*, 258).

Takmak, 'to pour melted metals into a mould', (Ḥajj, VII, 91).

Néshan, *nayshan*, 'to betroth', (Wood, 475); 'to aim at a target', (Sām, 191; Erwin, *A Short Reference*, 78; Mac, I, 421); 'to mark', (Gīl, 268; Bak, 490), Arm, *ménéshōnéh*, (YM I, *Hebrew-Aramaic*, 269) < *nīshān*, 'a mark', 'a medal', Tur, Per, 'same', (DH, *Qāmūs*, 287), 'to pin a medal on s.o.'s chest', (Cha, *Kalimāt*, 194; TA, 74).

Pahraz, as in *pahraz nafsah*, 'he imposed a diet on himself', *tpahraz*, 'to go on a diet', (Mac, I, 409, 436; Ḥana, *Mu'jam*, I, 709) < Tur, Per, *parhīz*, 'abstinence' (from food), (Stein, 246; ʿUbaydī, 42).

Parçam, *barçam* and *barjam*, 'to rivet', fig. 'to make a case light', (Mac, I, 416); 'to take care of once and for all' (an issue or a matter), as in *parçamhā l-qaḍiyyah*, (Wood, 51), 'he closed the matter successfully', (Mac, I, 425; Ḥana, *Mu'jam*, I, 686; Sām, 154; Bak, 103; DH, *Qāmūs*, 30; Cha, *Kalimāt*, 29; MM, 63); Tur, *perçīn*, Per, *perçīm*, 'rivet'.

Pardakh, *bardagh*, < Per, *pardākhtan*, 'to polish', (TA, 9; DH, *Qāmūs*, 38; Bak, 103), 'to shave the face', (Wood, 52), 'to shave and cut the hair completely with a razor' (fig.), (Bak, 103; Ḥana, *Mu'jam*, I, 687) < Per, *pardākhtan*. Note the Baghdadi expression, *pardakhūh*, 'they killed him', (Cha, *Kalimāt*, 30).

Pargal, *barkal*, 'to draw dividers' < Per, *purgal*, Tur, *pergel*, 'a pair of compasses', (Wood, 527); 'to manage matters' (fig.), (Cha, *Kalimāt*, 30; DH, *Qāmūs*, 38).

Pashwan, 'to install s.o. as a pasha', (Ḥajj, *al-Amthāl*, 143; Ḥana, *Mu'jam*, I, 695).

Pashwar, 'to be confused when talking', 'to speak nonsense' < Per, *paçvāra*, 'a piece of rug', (Ḥana, *Mu'jam*, I, 30)

Qapraç, *qapraj*, 'to be dry and wrinkled' (fabric), (Bak, 379).

Qōbaç, *qōpaç*, 'to button', 'to fasten, tie', (Bak, 399), *qōpça*, OTur, 'hook and eyes'.

Shaflaḥ, *falaḥa* ('Awwād, 24), the *sh* is prefix, 'to expose to cold air' (tr.).

Shalban, 'to climb up', (Wood, 247); 'to beautify', Tur, *çelebi*, 'nice, polite person'.

Shalman, 'to brag', 'to exaggerate', (Wood, 248).

Shalqaḥ, ('Awwād, 24), 'to toss on the ground' (tr.).

Shalṭagh, 'to trick, cheat' (in a game, accounts, etc.), OTur, *shalṭāq*, 'cheating', (Thin, 59; Shāl, II, 217); 'to deceive', (Wood, 247; MM, 336; YD, *Sefat*, 122; Gīl, 128; Mac, I, 216, 425; Sām, 167).

Shalwaṭ, 'to burn', 'to roast'.

Ṭakhmagh, 'to pitch a tent with a hammer' < OTur, *ṭoqmāq*, 'a wooden hammer with a big head', 'a door-knocker', *mṭakhmagh*, 'an affluent person', (Bak, 319), 'a huge person with a big head', (Cha, *Kalimāt*, 184); *mṭakhmagh* is said about a furnished home or a rich person (Bak, 318).

Ṭarsham, 'to become dark' < Per, *ṭār+shabb*, 'a dark night', (Shīr, 112).

Tashlaq, 'to lie down on one's back stretching out the arms and legs', (Bak, 122).

Ṭarjam, 'to be angry', (Ḥana, *al-Alfaẓ*, 233).

Warmak, 'to give away', 'to contribute' < Tur, *vermek*, 'to give', 'to pay the account for s.o.', as in *difa'it 'aléh wér* (lit. 'I paid the account for him'), i.e. 'I treated him', (MM, 231) < OTur, *ver*, 'give!', 'offer!' asking the waiter in a coffee shop to offer a guest something to drink, (Turj, 46).

Warnash, 'to varnish', Tur, *vernik*, 'lacquer', or Eng, 'to varnish'.

Zarkash, 'to decorate with embroidered golden designs', Per, *zar+kash*, 'covered with golden thread', (Ḥajj, *al-Amthāl*, 243; Thin, 91; Wood, 203; TA, 32).

D. 1.2. English

English words entered IA vocabulary mainly during the British occupation and Mandate in Iraq (1917–24). The following are such quadriradical verbs in IA:

Alman, more commonly *t'almān*, 'to become German' < *al-almān*, 'the Germans'.

Amrak, 'to make s.o. adopt the customs and manners of Americans', (Wood, 15), *t'amrak*, 'to act like an American', (Mac, I, 436).

Anglaz, *galnaz*, 'to anglicize'< *inglīzī*, *inglīz*, 'English people'.

Atmat, 'to automate', (MM, 339).

Balwas, 'to put on a blouse', (Ḥana, *Mu'jam*, I, 594), *z* > *s*.

Bawnas, 'to give a bonus', (Ḥana, *Mu'jam*, I, 626).

Dōbal, 'to double', (Bak, 213).

Fabrak, 'to fabricate', (MM, 339).

Farmal, 'to put the brake on'< *farmalah*, 'a car brake', (EB, 768).

Farnaj, 'to westernize' < *ifranjī*, 'European', (Sām, 190), *tfarnaj*, 'to adopt the customs of westerners', (Thin, 253; Wood, 351).

Fastar, *tfastar*, 'to become disappointed' < frustration, (MM, 232).

Ghalwan, 'to galvanize', (Sām, 187).

Hadraj, 'to pass hydrogen through s.th.', (Sām, 187).

Jalfan, 'to galvanize'.

Jangal, said figuratively about an uncivilized person as if he/she lived in a jungle, < 'jungle', 'forest', (Ḥana, *al-Alfāẓ*, 79).

Kansal, 'to cancel', (MM, 337).

Nagraz ('Awwād, 25), 'to anglicize', *tnagraz*, 'to pretend to be a civilized British person', (Sām, 191; Ḥana, *Mu'jam*, II, 124), 'to adopt English customs', where *l* > *r*, (MM, 334, Thin, 253).

Narvaz 'to make angry', < 'nerve', *tnarvaz*, 'to become angry', (Ḥana, *Mu'jam*, II, 122; MM, 300).

Pançar and *banjar*, 'to have a flat tyre', (Ḥana, *Mu'jam*, I, 703; Turj, 35; Baz, 41), 'to run out of strength' (fig.), (YD, *Sefat*, 122; Shāl, I, 380), 'to break down', (Wood, 52), 'to cause failure' (slang).

Pōlash and *bōlash*, 'to polish', (Gīl, 205), 'to deceive by flattering and showing kindness' (fig.), (Ḥana, *Mu'jam*, I, 708).

Qanṣal, 'to appoint s.o. as a counsel'.

Sakrab, 'to become worn out, good for nothing', *sikrāb*, 'scrap'. This verb is attested in the Kuwaiti dialect as well, (Ḥana, *al-Alfāẓ*, 176), *tsakrab*, 'to become useless', (Sām, 189).

Shaftan, *shaftar*, 'to get s.o. into a bad fix', lit. 'to shaft s.o.' (vulg.) < *shaft*, 'a stick'.

Talfan, 'to telephone', (Ḥana, *Mu'jam*, II, 104).

Talvaz, 'to televize', (MM, 109; Thin, 266).

There is a host of quadriliteral verbs, some of which are noticed in written Arabic only, like *raskala*, 'to recycle', *halwasa*, 'to hallucinate', *aksada*, 'to oxidize', *fabraka*, 'to manufacture, fabricate', (EB, 741), *tafalwar*, 'to fluoresce' < *filur*, 'fluorine', *tmalgham*, 'to amalgamate', (EB, 742), *halban*, 'to hellenize', (EB, 744).

French

Bastar, *pastar* < 'to pasteurize' < Louis Pasteur, a French chemist and bacteriologist (Sām, 187; Wood, 52; MM, 299).

Fanṭaz/s (Fr. *fantaisie*) < 'to decorate', 'to imagine', (FM, 431; Sām, 190; Bak, 431) 'to be indifferent', as in *fanṭaz 'alā-l-'ālam*, 'he did not give a damn about the world'.

Farnas, 'to make s.o. French', more commonly *tfarnas*, 'to become like the French', (Sām, 190).

Qōmas, 'to take commission', Fr. *commission* (Baz, 136).

Italian

Kartan, 'to stay in quarantine', Ita, *quarantine*, lit. 'forty' [days] during which no one is allowed to enter an area inflicted with a plague (TA, 62; Thin, 142).

Podar, *bodar*, 'to powder'.

Qanṭar, *qanṭagh*, 'to contract', (Wood, 379; Thin, 133) < Ita, *qrantratu*.

Sōban, 'to wash with soap' < *sapone*, (TA, 43).

Sōgar, *ṣōgar* and *sōkar*, 'to insure', (Ita, *assicurare*, *sicurta*), (TA, 38; MM, 218; Dabb, 126; Bak, 273); 'to register' (mail) being recently used in IA (informal), *tsōgar*, 'to be insured', (Erwin, *A Short Reference*, 78; Dabb, 122).

Ṭalyan, 'to make s.o. Italian', *iṭṭalyan*, 'to become Italian' < *al-ṭilyān*, 'the Italians', (EB, 763).

Greek

Bayṭar, *béṭar*, ‘to shoe a horse or a cow’ < Gr, *ippiatros*, however, the √ BṬR exists in the CA, ‘to furnish with shoes’.

Falsaf, ‘to philosophize’ (said derogatory), (Wood, 360); ‘to speak learnedly or pompously without real knowledge’, (Erwin, *A Short Reference*, 80), ‘to scrutinize’, *tfalsaf*, ‘to act as if one is a philosopher’, (Thin, 116; YD, *Sefat*, 202) < *faylasūf*, ‘philosopher’.

Maghnaṭ, and *maghṭas*, ‘to magnetize’, (Sām, 187) < ‘magnet’, Gr, *magnatis*.

Nōmas, more commonly *tnōmas*, ‘to behave o.s.’, ‘to teach manners and respect for others’ < Gr, *nomos*; ‘to brag’, (Ḥana, *Mu'jam*, II, 125).

F. APPENDIX I

Verbs Type 1.2.1.2

'Aḍ'aḍ, 'to keep biting', < *'aḍḍa*, CA, 'to bite', (Mac, I, 415; Wood, 312).

'Ad'ad, 'to mourn' < *mé'adōdéh*, 'a professional mourner'.

'Af'af, 'to cry or speak loudly and angrily', a distortion of *'aw'aw*, 'to bark' √ 'WY (Bak, 341).

'Aṭ'aṭ, 'to give off a pleasant and strong fragrance' (flower), (Thin, 90), *'aṭṭa*, 'same'.

'At'at, 'to pull lightly and successively'< *'atta* (Bak, 333).

'Ak'ak, 'to become very fat', *'ikka*, 'fat'.

Ba'ba', 'to bubble, gush out', CA; Arm, *mébaqbōqéh*, (YM I, *Hebrew-Aramaic*, 54); 'to bleat' (camel), Arm, *b'ībā*, 'a harsh sound', (Bak, 85).

Ba'ba', 'to say *bābā*' (papa), 'to repeat the sound *bā* repeatedly' CA, (Wright, I, 47).

Baçbaç, *bakbak*, 'to whine tearfully'< *bakā*, 'to weep', (Bak, 287), √ BKY; Arm, *mébakbōkéh*, (YM I, *Hebrew-Aramaic*, 187). Children in Basra use this verb in a game to mean, 'to heap bones on top of each other' < *tabakkā*, CA, 'to heap', (Dul, 54), *tbakbak*, 'to pretend to cry', (Sām, 199).

Baḥbaḥ, 'to add a little', (Mac, I, 415; Bak, 72), 'to let s.o. live well', (YD, *Sefat*, 182). *tbaḥbaḥ*, 'to be prosperous', 'to enjoy an easy life', (Gīl, 21; Bak, 72); 'to neigh', 'to clear one's throat', 'to sweep', (Mac, I, 415; Syr, FM, 35–6). In children's language *baḥḥ* means 'no more', 'nothing remains' (food), however in CA *biḥbāḥ*, 'abundance', (AF, *Mu'jam*, 5).

Baghbagh, 'to give s.th. secretly', (Bak, 85), *tbaghbagh*, 'to be confused and screaming', (Bak, 112).

Bahbah, 'to praise'< Per, *pah pah*, an expression of praise, (Cha, *Kalimāt*, 34).

Bakhbakh, ('Awwād, 22), 'to snore loudly' < *bakhkha*, CA, 'to snore'; 'to spray water', (YD, *Sefat*, 59).

Balbal, 'to moisten' < *balla*, 'to wet', CA; 'to drip', √ BLL, as in *balbal il-brīg*, 'the pot dripped' < *balbūlah*, 'spout', (Ḥana, *Mu'jam*, I, 585); 'to confuse', (Rabīn, 151; Soko, 220; Ben-Jacob, *Hebrew and Aramaic*, 52), Arm, *mébōlboléh*, (YM II, *Aramaic-Kurdish*, 217).

Balbaṣ, 'to open the eye while sleeping', (Bak, 90; MM, 62); Arm, *blaṣ*, (Cha, *Ath*, 46).

Baqbaq, 'to make the sound, *baq baq*' (hen), 'to speak a lot', (Bak, 76, 89); 'to bubble', (Ḥana, *Mu'jam*, I, 569; Sām, 197), 'to have blisters', ('Ubaydī, 48) < Arm, *baqbūqah*, 'a blister'; *mébaqbōqéh*, see *méba'bō 'éh*, (YM I, *Hebrew-Aramaic*, 54).

Barbar, 'to jabber', *Ḥanẓal*, 87; Bak, 75); 'to be angry', (YD, *Sefat*, 158; 'to be blistered', Ḥana, *Mu'jam*, I, 178).

Baṣbaṣ, 'to peep', (Cha, *Ath*, 20; Gīl, 278); 'to wag' (tail of a dog), (Wood, 35); 'to steal a look at s.o.' (Soko, 228; Mac, I, 423; YD, *Sefat*, 201), *tbaṣbaṣ*, 'to yield' (al-Karmilī, *Majmū'ah*, I, 264, n. 4); 'to close the lips and stick them out drawing air and making a sound similar to chirping' < Arm, *ṣwaṣ*, 'to chirp'.

Bashbash, 'to speak in a low pitch', 'to whisper' < *washwash*, *w* > *b*, (Gīl, 24; Cha, *Kalimat*, 32) < Per, *pushpūshah*, 'whispering'.

Baṭbaṭ, 'to become blistered', 'to swell'; (Wood, 37; YD, *Sefat*, 59; Ḥana, *Mu'jam*, I, 534), 'to crumble and turn into sop', 'to become full of holes' (fabric), (al-Karmilī, *Majmū'ah*, II, 167). In children's language, 'to bounce a ball'; (Ḥajj, VI, 105; 'Ubaydī, 49). It is likely that children invented this verb from *ṭōbah*, 'ball', IA, or < *ṭabṭab*, 'to pat'.

Bazbaz, 'to bubble', 'to become fermented and swollen', (Gīl, 23; Mac, I, 415; Ḥana, *Mu'jam*, I, 510), 'to dart' (eyes), (Wood, 33) < *bibīz*, 'a cemetery rat', which looks avidly for a prey at dark, 'to gush out', 'to appear (pimples) on the body' < CA, *bazza*, 'same', or composition of *bazagh+nabara*; 'to scatter', ('Ubaydī, 48, Bak, 80), √ BZZ, Syr, *bazbūzah*, 'swelling'.

Çabçab, 'to spill here and there', (Mac, I, 425), 'to splash' < *kabba*, CA, 'to pour', (Ḥana, *Mu'jam*, II, 272; Wood, 83), 'to drip', *méçapçōbéh* (YM I, *Hebrew-Aramaic*, 290).

Çakçak, 'to fall on the end of a bone', children's speech when playing *ç'āb* (a children's game with bones); 'to prick', (Ḥana, *Mu'jam*, II, 297; Mac, I, 418), 'to rattle', (YD, *Sefat*, 227), *tçakak*, 'to get pricked', (Mac, I, 431).

Çalçal, 'to overshadow', 'to become heavy upon', (Mac, I, 415); 'to provide a *ẓill* (shadow)', (Ḥana, VII, 83, n.15), as in the verse of an old Iraqi folk song, *çalçal 'alayya-r-rummān, nūmī fiza' lī*, 'the pomegranates protected me (lit. 'provided shade for me') and the sweet lemons came to help me'. The pomegranates stand for a women's breasts and the sweet lemons for the cheeks of the beloved' < *kalkala*, CA, < *kala'a*, 'to provide shade', (Yahuda, 409[77]; Ḥajj, VII, 83, n. 15; al-Karmilī, *Majmū'ah*, II, 54, n. 28).

---

77 Abraham Shalom Ezekiel Yahuda, 'Bagdadische Sprichwörter', in *Orientalische Theodor Nöldeke* (Giessen 1906), 399–416, (henceforth Yahuda).

Çaqçaq, 'to rattle', 'to knock', (Ben-Jacob, *Hebrew and Aramaic*, 171) < *çaqq*, IA, 'to collide' (in a game of marbles), (Ḥajj, II, 141), 'to produce a sound similar to that of burning oil', (Sām, 197).

Ḍa'ḍa', ('Awwād, 23), 'to weaken', (Bak, 123; Sām, 198), 'to shake' (a man or a position); (Mac, I, 415) < CA.

Da'da', 'to run in a heavy pace', 'to wobble', *tda'da'a*, 'to have a tottering gait'.

Dabdab, 'to crawl a lot' (child) < *dabba*, CA, 'same', (DH, *Qāmūs*, 105), 'to grow up fat like a *dubb* (bear)', said of a growing child (Ḥana, *Mu'jam*, III, 24), 'to become roly-poly', (Mac, I, 418; Bak, 212, 458).

Dafdaf, 'to play the tambourine' < *daff*, 'tambourine', (Wood, 161).

Dagdag, 'to grow a *digdigah*' (IA, 'a growth in the eye'), 'to pinch', (Gīl, 88); 'to crack', 'to rap', 'to pound', (Erwin, *A Short Reference*, 78).

Daghdagh, Arm, 'to tickle', ('Ubaydī, 185; Mac, I, 418; Wood, 371; Qad, III, 102), *itdaghdagh*, 'to be ticklish', (Mac, I, 432; Gīl, 88).

Dahdah and *dahdā* √ DHW, 'to roll', 'to push', (Ḥana, *Mu'jam*, III, 112).

Daḥdaḥ, 'to become roly-poly', (Mac, I, 418; Ḥana, *Mu'jam*, III, 32); 'to waddle', (Wood, 153), *mdaḥdaḥ*, 'stocky', 'a short-statured person', (Gīl, 88; YD, *Sefat*, 112).

Dakdak, 'to tickle', (Mosul) < *daghdagh*, CA, Arm, (Ghanīmah, 268; Bak, 222), 'to sing like a rooster', 'to crow' < *dīk*, 'a rooster'.

Dakhdakh, 'to cause dizziness', 'to give s.o. a headache' < *dākh*, IA, 'to pass out, 'to faint', √ DWKh.

Daldal, 'to lower', CA, √ DLW; 'to thin'< Syr, *dlīl*, 'thin', (Kāmil, 64).

Damdam, 'to mutter', 'to grumble', (Mac, I, 425; Bak, 224; Sām, 197, 161).

Dandan, 'to buzz', 'to hum *dan dan* softly', (Gīl, 93; YD, *Sefat*, 163), In CA *dandana*, 'to complain', 'to cry out', 'to murmur (rebelliously)' < *danna*, 'to be annoyed, fed up'.

Daqdaq, 'to bang continuously', 'to pound many times', 'to crush into powder', (Cha, *Ath*, 41), 'to tattoo' (slang), (Ḥana, *Mu'jam*, III, 72; Bak, 222); 'to scrutinize'; (Ben-Jacob, *Hebrew and Aramaic*, 102); 'to be fussy, particular', (Wood, 161).

Dardar, 'to plant', 'to scatter seeds' < *dharra*, (DH, *Qāmūs*, 107), *dh* > *d*.

Dawdaw, 'to stutter because of anger', (Gīl, 94; YD, *Sefat*, 159, 'to make a sound like that of worms'< *dūd*, 'to become worm-eaten', *dawwād*, 'same', (Wood, 168), 'to talk nonsense', 'to mumble', (Ḥana, *Mu'jam*, III, 98).

Dhabdhab, 'to throw here and there', 'to toss', *dhabb*, 'to throw', (Wood, 174; Erwin, *A Short Reference*, 79); 'to fluctuate', (Ḥajj, *al-Amthal*; 220; Gīl, 88).

Faḍfaḍ, 'to become vast', CA < *faḍā'*, 'space', (Sām, 196).

Fajfaj, 'to slice, cut' < *fajja* 'to split', (Mez, 253).

Fakfak, 'to take apart', (Erwin, *A Short Reference*, 79), *fakk*, 'to break open' (a seal), 'to open', 'to 'unscrew', 'to turn on', 'to untie', (Wood, 135 and 358).

Falfal, 'to 'torture', (Mac, I, 415), *tfalfal*, 'to cry bitterly', 'to become curly', 'to be slightly piquant', Arm, *ithpalpal*, 'to cry bitterly' (baby), (Bak, 125); Arm, (Cha, *Ath*, 26); 'to be tantalized', (Mac, I, 432).

Faqfaq, 'to boil' (pot), 'to gush out', (DH, *Qāmūs*, 213), *faqqa*, CA, 'to get blisters'.

Fardash, 'to scatter here and there' (furniture), (Thin. 110).

Farfar, 'to tear up' (said of an animal), (Shīr, 119) < Per, *para para*, 'piece by 'piece', 'to shake itself' (bird) , CA, 'to cry one's heart out', 'to become exhausted from crying', (Wood, 350); 'to throw here and there', (Gīl, 196). Note the expressions *farfar adhānu*, 'he listened carefully', (Bak, 360); and 'to move and hit the ground when it is slaughtered' (bird. chicken), (Thin, 111).

Farfas, 'to grow pimples', 'to break wind without noise', *fasfūsah*, CA, *fasā*, 'same', √ FSW, *fasw*, Per, 'whispering', 'humming'; 'to dwindle' (fire, light), (Bak, 374).

Fashfash, 'to deflate' < *fashsh*, 'to shrink back', (Wood, 353; Baz, 125; Qad, II, 121), 'to be empty' < *fashūsh*, 'empty', (MM, 227).

Fatfat (tr.) < *fatta* or < *fattat*, 'to break into small pieces', (Bak, 343; DH, *Qāmūs*, 210; ʿUbaydī, 54; Shal, II, 92, n. 6), CA, *tfatfat*, 'to crumble', Arm, *pathpath*, (Cha, *Ath*, 67); 'to get on one's nerves' as in *ibniç ma-yinḥimil wi-fatfit il-galub*, 'your son is unbearable and gets on one's nerves', lit. 'your son is unbearable and he cuts the heart into small pieces', (Wood, 343).

Faṭfaṭ, 'to gurgle', 'to make a sucking noise', 'to decompose', (Wood, 356), 'to suck out water and air from a tube or a pipe', said of s.o. who speaks incoherently; 'to make sounds (woman) when having intercourse' (vulg.), (Thin, 115).

Fazfaz, 'to get up scared' < *fazza*, 'to get up suddenly', (Bak, 363).

Gabgab, 'to stick out' (breasts), (al-Karmilī, *Majmūʿah*, II, 241, n. 7) < *gabb*, 'to swell', 'to bulge', (Wood, 383).

Gaḏgḏaḏ, 'to shiver because of cold', (ʿUbaydī, 54; Bak, 433), < Arm, *gadhgadh*, 'to shrink from cold', (Cha, *Ath*, 76).

Galgal, 'to wiggle', 'to shake', (Wood, 39) , 'to make curly'(hair), 'to make into a ball-like shape', (YD, *Sefat*, 204; YM II, *Aramaic-Kurdish*, 23); 'to revolve', 'to tilt the bucket in order to fill it with water', (Thin, 175); 'to roll down' < *galgāl*, Heb, 'wheel', *gilgél*, Heb, 'to roll down', (Ben-Jacob, *Hebrew and Aramaic*, 36).

Gaʿgas, 'to shrink', 'to wither', (Bak, 433).

Gangan, 'to play an instrument lightly and sing in a very low voice', (Thin, 179); 'to complain', 'to prattle', (Gīl, 60; YD, *Sefat*, 159).

Gargar, 'to blabber', (Mac, I, 415).

Gaṣgaṣ, 'to cut up', (Mac, I, 415; Sam 119; Cha, *Ath*, 71; Erwin, *A Short Reference*, 78) < *qaṣṣa*, CA, 'same', *tgaṣgaṣ*, 'to be clipped', (Mac, I, 431), 'same', (Cha, *Ath*, 27).

Gashgash, *qashqash*, 'to collect s.th. in a hurry', (Thin, 166) < *gashsh*, 'to amass', 'to take off the top', (Wood, 389); Heb, *qishqésh*, 'to collect firewood', *qashsh*, 'to sweep', *qishqāshah*, 'a broom made of straw', (Gīl, 213).

Gazgaz, 'to bite', 'to grit (the teeth) because of anger' (Wood, 388; 'Ubaydī, 54; Thin, 165; Shāl, III, 545) < Per, *gazīdān* < 'to bite', or *gazzah*, 'a bite', (MM, 265; Cha, *Kalimāt*, 173; Bak, 432; Ḥajj, III, 181[78]); 'to become dry and shrunk' < *kazūzah*, 'dryness and shrinkage', (Cha, *Ath*, 75).

Ghabghab, 'to become fat', 'to live comfortably' (fig.), Gīl, 183, 'to bulge', 'to swell'; (Wood, 383), 'to curdle' (milk, yogurt), *mghabghib*, 'fat', 'curdled', (YD, *Sefat*, 248).

Ḥalḥal, 'to wiggle, jiggle', 'to budge', (Wood, 114), 'to loosen one's clothes and relax', *ḥalla*, 'to untie' or 'to unscrew', (Sām, 198; Ḥana, *Mu'jam*, II, 399), *taḥalḥal*, 'to move over', (Bak, 175; Ḥajj, *al-Amthāl*, 172); Arm, *mékhalkhōléh*, (YM I, *Hebrew-Aramaic*, 155).

Jarjar, 'to jerk or pull back and forth', 'to pull repeatedly', CA, 'to haggle' (Mac, I, 415; Thin, 84, n. 23; DH, *Qāmūs*, 76; Gīl, 339; Wood, 69; Bak, 142), *jarra*, 'to pull a lot', (Cha, *Ath*, 30). In negotiating the price of goods, the epithet, *arr w-jarr*, 'bargaining back and forth' is common; 'to blabber', (Mac, I, 418). Usually, this verb is used in the expression, *yijarjir wiy'ar'ir*, 'he haggled', (Bak, 142; Mac, 418); 'to blackmail' (fig.), (YD, *Sefat*, 206). Note the epithet, *ṣār bénhūm 'arr u-jarr*, 'they quarrelled', lit. 'there was pulling and pushing between them', (Thin, 84, n. 23).

Ghadghad, 'to become curdled', (YD, *Sefat*, 46); 'to grow glands or bulges' < *ghuddah*, 'a gland', 'to become sour' (milk), ('Ubaydī, 54).

Ghalghal, 'to penetrate', 'to pass through', (Wood, 338); *mékhalkhōléh*, (YM I, *Hebrew-Aramaic*, 257), Heb, *hilhel*, 'same' (water).

Ghazghaz, 'to over-beautify', (Shāl, II, 118), *tghzghaz*', 'to beautify s.o. too much', (Ḥana, *Mu'jam*, II, 81).

78 'Azīz al-Ḥajjiyyah, *Baghdādiyyāt* III (1973), (henceforth Ḥajj, III).

Gamgam, 'to be incomprehensible', 'to stammer', (Sām, 198), Heb, *gimgém*, (YD, *Sefat*, 159; Ben-Jacob, *Hebrew and Aramaic*, 37), Arm, *gamgém*.

Gharghar, 'to gurgle', (Mac I, 415) < *garra*, 'to fill the mouth with water', CA, (Wright, I, 47), *mégharghōréh* (YM I, *Hebrew-Aramaic*, 76).

Ḥabḥab, ('Awwād, 23), 'to produce grain seeds', 'to get pimples' < *ḥabb*, 'seeds'. This verb is used as the epithet, 'to rush', (Wood, 46).

Habhab, 'to ventilate'< *habba*, 'to blow' (air, wind), (Wood, 467), Arm, *méhabhōbéh*, (YM I, *Hebrew-Aramaic*, 94), 'to inflame', (YM I, *Hebrew-Aramaic*, 230), *mhabhab*, 'wide' (dress), (Ḥajj, IV, 135).

Ḥadḥad, 'to sharpen' (knife), 'to set a boundary' < *ḥadd*, 'limit', 'piquant' (wine), hence 'to become acid-like'.

Hadhad, 'to roll from up to down' < *hadd*, 'to let go of', (Thin, 270); 'to release', (Wood, 478); 'to weaken'; (Sām, 198), *mhadhad*, 'wobbling' (tooth), (YD, *Sefat*, 62).

Hafhaf, 'to blow air or move air with a fan' < *mahaffah*, 'fan', or *haffa*, 'same', (Qaf, 613), 'to move the hands a lot when walking', 'to hit' < *haff*, 'same', 'to walk quickly', (YD, *Sefat*, 212; Wood, 481).

Hajhaj, 'to make s.o. go away', (al-Karmilī, *Majmū'ah*, I, 355, n. 1) < *hajja*, 'to stir up', 'to make s.o. tired deliberately', CA.

Ḥakḥak, 'to scratch a lot', 'to brush up against' < *ḥakka*, 'to scratch', (Wood, 104). This quadriradical verb is formed in order to distinguish between *ḥakka*, 'to rub' and *ḥakḥak*, 'to scratch, *tḥakḥak*, 'to scrape', 'to scratch o.s.', ('Ubaydī, 50), Arm, *mékharkhōkéh* (YM I, *Hebrew-Aramaic*, 260).

Halhal, 'to ululate', (Mac, I, 415; Sām, 197; Thin, 285).

Ḥamḥam, 'to neigh', 'to clear one's throat', (Ḥana, *Mu'jam*, II, 408; Mac, I, 415), 'to rustle', 'to repeat the syllable *ḥam* twice', 'to rise' (body temperature), (Bak, 179; YD, *Sefat*, 221) > *ḥumma*, 'fever', CA; 'to sweep', Arm, *ḥumḥama*, 'sweeping', (Cha, *Ath*, 89).

Hamham, 'to intend to do s.th.', *hamma*, CA, 'same', (Thin, 287).

Ḥanḥan, 'to be rotten and have a red or black colour' (inside almonds and other nuts), CA, < *ḥannan*, 'same', (*Muḥiṭ*, 199).

Harhar, 'to flow' (liquid), 'to leak', 'to scatter' (dry things) < Arm, *harhér*, 'same', (Cha, *Ath*, 87).

Ḥarḥar, 'to start a quarrel', (Avīshūr, 222).

Ḥaṣḥaṣ, 'to make a crunching sound in the mouth as if crushing grains or sand', (Bak, 503); 'to reveal' (truth).

Ṣahṣah, ‘to say *ṣah* many times’, ‘shut up!’ (Ben-Jacob, *Hebrew and Aramaic*, 46).

Ḥasḥas, ‘to whisper’ < *hashasah*, ‘a very low voice’, ‘whispering’, (Ḥana, *Mu'jam*, II, 364).

Ḥasḥas, ‘to touch trying to feel s.th.’ < CA, *ḥassa*, ‘to feel’.

Hashhash, ‘to keep a child amused’, (Bak, 503; Thin, 282). In CA, *hashhasha*, ‘to move s.th.’.

Ḥashḥash, ‘to smoke a lot of hashish’, (Ḥana, *Mu'jam*, II, 371).

Ḥaṭḥaṭ, to be scarce’, ‘to be stingy’, CA, ‘same’. This verb is also attested in the Lebanese dialect, (AF, *Mu'jam*, 32).

Hawhaw, ‘to make noise’, ‘to dance’. The verb is derived from a slaves’ dance, (Ḥana, *al-Alfāẓ*, 404), ‘to hesitate’, ‘to feel doubt’, (Wood, 505).

Ḥazḥaz, ‘to loathe’ < *ḥazāzah*, ‘rancour’, ‘enmity’, CA, (Wood, 100).

Hazhaz, ‘to swing’ (tr.), ‘to shake in order to settle particles and dirt in the bottom of a sieve’, (Mac, I, 425; Sām, 198) < *hazza*, ‘to rock’, ‘to agitate’ √ HZZ.

Ja'ja', ‘to speak loudly’, (Ḥana, *Majmū'ah*, II, 211) < *je'ū*, ‘a loud bellow made by an ox’, Syr, *j'a*, Heb, *ga'a*, (MF, 101), ‘to bellow’ (bull), > CA.

Jabjab, ‘to cause to be timid and afraid’, (YD, *Sefat*, 156), *tjabjab*, ‘to become introverted’, (Wood, 66; Bak, 115; Ḥana, *Mu'jam*, II, 32), *jabba*, CA, ‘to cut’.

Jafjaf, ‘to dry’ (tears), (al-Karmilī, *Majmū'ah*, I, 246, n. 4) < *jaffa*, ‘to become dry’, CA.

Jaghjagh, ‘to blackmail gradually’ (fig.), (Gīl, 339).

Jahjah, ‘to become clear’ (sky), ‘to dilute’, √ JHY, CA < Arm, *gahgah*, ‘to illuminate’, ‘to become clear’, (Cha, *Ath*, 33), ‘to appear’ (sun, light, dawn). In Mosul people say *jahjahit ḥālutu*, ‘his condition has improved’, and *jahjah wuçço*, ‘the signs of paleness and sickness disappeared from his face’, lit. ‘his condition has become clear’, (Bak, 150). Note also *jahjar*, ‘to be clear from clouds’, ‘to appear’ (dawn), (Ḥana, *Mu'jam*, II, 254), CA, ‘same’.

Jaljal, ‘to ring’ < *jinjil* (Bak, 145) < *juljul*, CA, ‘a small bell’, (TA, 21; Cha, *Kalimāt*, 326) < *laqlāq*, CA, ‘tongue’, ‘to use the sound *q* a lot when talking’, (Sām, 197); ‘to lick < CA, *laqqa*, ‘same’.

Gaḥgaḥ, ‘to cough’, (Wood, 384); *méqaḥqōḥéh*’, (YM I, *Hebrew-Aramaic*, 294).

Ka'ka', ‘to obstruct the path of s.o.’, (Thin, 145) *ka''a*, CA, ‘same’, *tka'ka'*, ‘to tear’, (al-Karkhī, *Dīwān*, III, 382, n. 1).

Kabkab, ‘to make s.th. round’, ‘to round into a small ball’, (Piamenta, II, 424; Baz, 140; DH, *Qāmūs*, 231; Sām, 198).

Kaçkaç, *kashkash*, 'to shoo away, expel' (animals) < 'to say *kish* repeatedly', (Wood. 406); < Arm, *mékashkōshé*, (MY, II, 261); 'to rise' (dough), (Bak, 413); Arm, *kashkésh*, 'to hem the end of a dress', (Baz, 143); 'to wag' (tail), 'shake', Per, *kashīdan*, 'to pull'.

Kadhkadh, 'to shiver from cold' < Arm, *kadhkadh*, (Cha, *Ath*, 76).

Kafkaf 'an, 'to stop', 'prevent', (al-Karmilī, *Majmū'ah*, I, 349), CA, 'same', *mékafkōféh*, 'to be angry', (YM I, *Hebrew-Aramaic*, 259).

Kalkal, 'to provide a shade', *kala'a*, CA, 'same', (Yahuda, 409). See also *çalçal*.

Karkar, 'to burst into loud laughter', (YD, *Sefat*, 239; DH, *Qāmūs*, 235). 'to keep guffawing', (Mac, I, 418; Bak, 408; Thin, 143; Gīl, 226). It is also attested in Hebrew as *kirkér*, (Ben-Jacob, *Hebrew and Aramaic*, 91).

Kaskas, 'to plead' < *kuskus*, 'hem of a dress' (*kashkūshah*), (Sām, 196) > *kassa*, (tr.), 'to pound', 'to curse the private part of a woman' (*kuss*, *virgiena*).

Kazkaz, 'to be inflicted with *kuzāz*, 'tetanus', 'to be dry and contracted', (Cha, *Ath*, 76).

Khadkhad, ('Awwād, 23), 'to become red on one side of the face'. In CA, 'to plant in groves', *khudd*, 'furrows'.

Khaḍḍkhaḍ, 'to shake with vigour', (Wood, 137), 'to agitate', *khaḍḍa*, CA, 'to vibrate', 'to masturbate', (Shāl, I, 368).

Khalkhal, 'to weaken', 'to juggle', 'to become sour like *khal* (vinegar)', (Gīl, 81; Wood, 141; YD, *Sefat*, 40); 'to shake'; *tkhalkhal*, CA, 'to become loose'.

Khamkham, 'to become spoiled' (food), (Ḥana, *Mu'jam*, II, 527), 'to smell bad' (food), (Gīl, 82; Wood, 145); < *khamma*, CA, 'to check', 'to stink'; 'to look carefully' < Arm, *ḥumā*, 'to look and inspect', (Cha, *Ath*, 37), *mkhamkhim*, 'stinky', 'humid' (weather), (Gīl, 245; YD, *Sefat*, 275).

Khankhan, 'to speak nasally', (Mac, I, 415) < *khunnah*, 'nasal twang', CA, or *khanna*, 'same', (Wood, 147; Ḥana, *Mu'jam*, II, 531).

Kharkhar, 'to run heavily' (nose), (Ḥana, *Mu'jam*, II, 479; Mac, I, 425) < *kharr*, 'to ooze', (Wood, 132), 'to murmur' (water), Arm, *ḥirḥīr*, and *kharīr*, CA, 'the murmur of running water'.

Kashkash, 'to drive away an animal', 'to shoo', (Wood, 406; Ḥajj, IV, 263) < *kishsh*, an Aramaic word for driving away animals, Aramaic *mékōshkōshéh* (YM I, *Hebrew-Aramaic*, 261), or < *kashīdan*, Per, 'to pull the hem of the dress in order to decorate it with a stripe', (Cha, *Kalimāt*,183; DH, *Qāmūs*, 236; Wood, 226; Baz, 147), 'to rise' (dough), (Bak, 413).

Khashkhash, 'to rattle like a *khashkhashah* (rattle), (YD, *Sefat*, 48), CA, 'same', (Wright, I, 47); 'to make a noise' (said of solid items like money etc.), (YM II,

Aramaic-Kurdish, 259), (Wood, 132; Gīl, 76), *tkhashkhash*, 'to intermingle with people easily'; *khashsh*, IA, 'to enter', (Ḥana, *Mu'jam*, II, 496); 'to shrink', as in *hal-i-qmāsh yikhush bil-ghasil*, 'This fabric shrinks when washed', (Wood, 135).

Khaṣkhaṣ, 'to privatize' (a recent coinage); (EB, 764) < *khaṣṣa*, CA.

La'la', 'to boom', (Gīl, 237; Mac, I, 415), 'to speak in a thunderous voice', 'to make an irritatingly loud noise', √ LW'; 'to sound like fired bullets', (Sām, 197); 'to stutter', (Ben-Jacob, *Hebrew and Aramaic*, 97).

Lablab, 'to bloom', 'to blossom', Heb, *libléb*, (Ben-Jacob, *Hebrew and Aramaic*, 93); 'to extract the core', (Wood, 417) < *lub*, 'core', 'centre', (Bak, 439); 'to polish' (wheat rice); 'to clear up a matter' (fig.), (Thin, 185, n. 8); 'to peel and cut' (watermelon), (Thin, 184).

Ladhladh, *tladhladh li*, 'to go around s.o. imploring', (Thin, 189).

Laflaf, 'to wrap many times', 'to envelop', 'to wipe s.th.', 'to beat about the bush', (Mac, I, 415; Gīl, 238; YD, *Sefat*, 237); 'to hide' or 'to embezzle' used as an epithet, (Ḥajj, *al-Amthāl*, 224); 'to cheat', (Shāl, II, 645); 'to take possession of others', (Sām, 152); 'to eat a lot' (vulg.), (Thin, 193); *tlaflaf*, 'to wrap o.s.', 'to be taken away', i.e. 'stolen, pinched', (Mac, I, 432).

Laghlagh, 'to prattle', 'to talk nonsense', (BY), 93 < *lajlaj*, 'to talk a lot', 'to stutter', (Mac, I, 436; Bak, 131), *ithlaghlagh*, 'to pester', (Cha, *Ath*, 27; Thin, 192); 'to move the tongue a lot', (Bak, 433).

Lahlah, ('Awwād 25), 'to stutter', (YM II, 261); *itlahlah*, Arm, *ithlahlah*, 'to be very thirsty and dry', (Cha, *Ath*, 27; Bak, 132).

Laḥlaḥ, 'to move' (intr.), (DH, *Qāmūs*, 246).

Lajlaj, 'to chatter', 'to nag' < *lajja* 'to persist', CA, 'to be a pest', *tlajlaj*, 'to stutter', (Mac, I, 427; Ḥajj, *al-Amthāl*, 116).

Lakhlakh, 'to emit a bad smell' (from wet clothes), (Cha, *Ath*, 177); 'to clutter'; 'to wet the hem of a dress', (Bak, 439); Heb, *likhlékh*, 'to dirty', (Ben-Jacob, *Hebrew and Aramaic*, 96), (Avīshūr, 226).

Laklak, 'to make and save a lot of money', Arm, *laklék*, (YD, *Sefat*, 237) < *luk*, 'a great number' (hundred of thousands in Hindu), (Ḥanẓal, 602; Thin, 194); 'to stain', 'to spatter', < *lakk*, Per, 'red wax', (Wood, 426; Cha, *Kalimāt*, 178; MM, 289).

Lamlam, 'to gather together', (Sām, 198; al-Karmilī, *Majmū'ah*, II, 300, n. 34; Bak, 446; Mac, I, 411), 'to collect', (Wood, 247; AF, *Mu'jam*, 198). Arm, *mélamlōméh*, (YM I, *Hebrew-Aramaic*, 264).

Laqlaq, 'to lick'< *laqqa*, CA, 'to flatter', 'to move the tongue when speaking', 'to prattle', (Bak, 443; Mac, 425; Gīl, 238; Ben-Jacob, *Hebrew and Aramaic*, 98; Baz, 160; Wood, 425).

Laṭlaṭ, 'to gobble', 'to become saturated with water or mud' (clothes), 'to drip water from wet clothes while walking', (Thin, 190; Bak, 440), 'to slosh over' as in *la-titris il-jidir tamām ḥatta maylaṭliṭ il-ḥalib*', 'don't fill the pot completely so the milk won't slosh over', (Wood, 422); 'to gobble up', (Mac, I, 418), *mlaṭlaṭ*, 'an epithet for s.th. or s.o. disgusted', (Ḥajj, *al-Amthāl*, II, 292; Shāl, III, 132; al-Karmilī, *Majmū'ah*, II, 300, n. 34).

Lazlaz, 'to look at s.th. while one's eyes are moving', (Thin, 189), 'to glance furtively at s.o.', 'to rush' (tr.); 'to appear' (crescent), (al-Karmilī, I, 125, n. 61).

Ma'ma', 'to make the sound *mā'mā*" (i.e. 'to bleat' like contented grazing sheep), (Ḥajj, II, 71; Thin, 218, n. 72; Shāl, III, 425) < CA.

Maçmaç, 'to kiss a lot' < *maç*, Per. 'a kiss' in children's language (Cha, *Kalimāt*, 181; Thin, 205).

Madhmadh, 'to lie', 'to decline to answer' (Thin, 207).

Maḍmaḍ and *makhmaḍ*, 'to rinse one's mouth', (DH, *Qāmūs*, 260; Wood, 441; Gīl, 248); 'to taste a little', (YD, *Sefat*, 42).

Makmak, *tmakmak*, 'to move s.o.', (Bak, 133). The following proverbs using this verb are said about a lazy and slow daughter-in-law (Mosul), *itmakmikī la-tākilkī -l samaki*, 'get up, lest the fish eat you' and *lamma titmakmak il-kannī yinghaliq bāb il-jannī*, 'when the daughter-in-law gets up (lit. moves) the gate of paradise will close', (Ghulāmī, 26, 120[79]).

Malmal, more commonly *tmalmal*, 'to move away a little', (Ḥana, *Mu'jam*, II,114).

Marmar, *maghmagh*, ('Awwād, 25), 'to cause pain and troubles', 'to embitter', (Wood, 437) < *murr'*, 'bitter', *tmarmar*, 'to be distressed and annoyed', (Mac, I, 418, 431); 'to be angry and upset', (DH, *Qāmūs*, 263; Baz, 166; Ḥana, *Mu'jam*, I, 110).

Mashmash, 'to feel and touch with one's hand', (Gīl, 248; YD, *Sefat*, 221), Arm, *mashmōshéh*, 'to pat', (YM I, *Hebrew-Aramaic*, 303; Wood, 439), *mashsh*, IA, 'to lap', 'to wipe off', 'to suck' (bone) , (Mac, I, 415).

Maṣmaṣ, 'to suck strongly'; 'to kiss', (mostly humorous), (Mac, I, 415; Gīl, 248; Wood, 440), 'to become hard to break a walnut's shell', (Thin, 74) < *maṣṣa*, CA, 'to suck'.

Matmat < *tamtam*, 'to stutter', (Thin, 205; Ḥana, *Mu'jam*, II, 108; Mac, I, 415).

79 Muḥammad al-Ghulāmī, *Kitāb al-Muraddad min al-Amthāl al-'Āmmiyyah al-Mawṣuliyyah* (Baghdad 1964), (henceforth Ghulāmī).

Maṭmaṭ, 'to stretch out the hands and legs', (Gīl, 248), 'to become weak or soft like rubber'; 'to haggle over an inconsequential matter', (Thin, 216; Mac, I, 415; Turj, 122) < *maṭmaṭa*, CA, 'same'.

Mazmaz, ('Awwād, 25), 'to sip', CA; Arm, *mizmōzéh*, (YM II, *Aramaic-Kurdish*, 242); 'to do s.th. silly', (Bak, 249).

Na'na', 'to become weak, unable', (Bak, 489); 'to break one's bone', (Sām, 198); 'to become fresh like mint leaves', (*Shīr*, 154); *tna'na'*, 'to sway', (Ḥajj, *al-Amthāl*, 205).

Nafnaf, 'to snuff a lot', *naffa*, 'to snuff', (Shīr, 154).

Naghnagh, 'to hum a tune', 'to coo', 'to talk softly (especially to a child)' < *nghā*, 'to moan repeatedly', (Wood, 464; Bak, 487) √ NGhY.

Nagnag, 'to peck at food', (Mac, I, 418; Ḥajj, V, 352), 'to eat a small amount', (Wood, 470; Shāl, III, 431; Thin, 251), 'to eat as little as a bird's beak can pick' < Per, *nūg*, 'beak', (Bak, 489; Cha, *Kalimāt*, 193; Thin, 246; Gīl, 267), 'to speak in a low voice due to dissatisfaction', (Tomā, 58), 'to be a pest' like the croaking (*naqīq*) of the frog (Turj, 56).

Nahnah, *tnahnah*, CA, 'to cough', 'to clear mucus from the throat', (Ḥana, *Mu'jam*, II, 121) , 'to move' (intr.), ('Ubaydī, 48), CA, 'same'.

Nakhnakh, 'to soak' (bread) in soup or water', (Thin, 237) < *nakhkh*, 'light rain', CA.

Namnam, 'to have delicate features' (child) < *nimnim*, 'very tiny and delicate beads for decorating a child's dress', (Wood, 472).

Naqnaq, 'to nag', 'to bother', (Mac, 415) < *naqīq*, 'croak of a frog', (Sām, 197), 'to become grumpy', (Gīl, 267; Wood, 468). See also *nagnag*.

Nashnash, 'to enjoy o.s.', 'to feel better', (Wood, 459); 'to recuperate', (Bak, 484, Ḥana, *Mu'jam*, 122), *tnashnash*, 'to feel better', *mnashnish*, an epithet for a well-off person (Ḥajj, *al-Amthāl*, 294).

Nawnaw, 'to whine', 'to meow', (DH, *Qāmūs*, 287; Bak, 489; YD, *Sefat*, 194).

Naznaz, ('Awwād, 25), 'to ooze', (Wood, 455) < *nazza*, 'to spill'; 'to pamper' < Per, *nāz*, pampering', (Cha, *Kalimāt*, 190), *tnaznaz*, 'to play hard to get'.

Paspas, (Cha, *Kalimāt*, 32); Per, *paspesandān*, 'whispering', (Ḥana, *Mu'jam*, I, 694); 'to be empty of contents' (said of nuts), (YD, *Sefat*, 45; Gīl, 205).

Pahpah, 'to praise' < Per. *bah bah*, an expression of appreciation, 'bravo!', (Cha, *Kalimāt*, 34; Ḥana, *Mu'jam*, I, 709).

Paqpaq, 'to hesitate and suspect' < Heb, *piqpéq* (Ben-Jacob, *Hebrew and Aramaic*, 121, 163).

Parpar, (Wood, 22) 'to dress s.o. in old clothes', (Bak, 102; Baz, 36) < Per, *parāpīr*, 'torn and worn out items', *mparpar*, 'one who wears shabby clothes' (Bak, 452).

Pashpash, 'to whisper' < *washwash*, (*w* > *b* > *p*), (Sām, 197; Bak, 82).

Paspas 'to whisper', < Per, *buçpuçah*, 'whispering', (Cha, *Kalimāt*, 32); 'to argue about trivial matters', (Shāl, III, 405); 'to break seeds with the teeth', (Sam 196); 'to prey', Syr, (FM, 432).

Qabqab, 'to click' (teeth), 'to shiver', 'to be infected' (wound) < *qabba*, 'same', (Bak, 378), 'to roar', (*Muḥīṭ*, 713).

Qaḍqaḍ, 'to crunch', 'to gnaw' (a bone) < *qaḍḍa*, CA, 'same'; 'to grit the teeth', (Shāl, II, 545; DH, *Qāmūs*, 222).

Qarqad, and *qafqaf*, 'to become dry', (DH, *Qāmūs*, 222; YD, *Sefat*, 248), < *qadda*, CA, 'same' < Arm, *qfad*, Heb, √ QFD.

Qafqaf, ('Awwād, 24), 'to shiver due to fever or coldness', (YD, *Sefat*, 190; Thin, 173) < *qaffa*, CA, 'same'.

Qaḥqaḥ, *gaḥgaḥ*, 'to cough repeatedly', (Bak, 382; Wood, 384; YD, *Sefat*, 58) < Arm, *ithqaḥqaḥ*, (Cha, *Ath*, 27) < CA, *qaḥḥa*, 'to cough'.

Qalqal, *galgal*, 'to move' (tr.), 'to shake a bucket in the water', (Thin 175); 'to worry', (Shāl, I, 317); *itqalqal*, 'to say unpleasant things', (Ben-Jacob, *Hebrew and Aramaic*, 178).

Qamqam, ('Awwād, 24), 'to complain', (Wehr, 790).

Qaṣgaṣ, 'to clip' (a bird's wings), (Ḥajj, *al-Amthāl*, 254, n. 5), 'to cut more than once', Arm, 'same'.

Qashmar, *kashmar*, *ghashmar* (Bedouins and southern villages), 'to fool', (Sām, 179; Gīl, 214; Bak, 388; Ḥajj, II, 85; IV, 221), 'to deceive', (Wood, 373; al-Karmilī, *Majmū'ah*, II, 222; Thin, 129; Mac, I, 421). This verb is used in the Gulf countries with the same meaning (Qaf, 460). In the south of Iraq, *q* > *k* (*kashmar*), Tur, *qashmér*, 'buffoon', *tqashmar*, 'to be fooled', (Mac, I, 432).

Qashqash, 'to pick up refuse', (Ḥana, *al-Alfāẓ*, 606), 'to collect quickly', (Thin, 166), 'to sweep', Arm, *qishqāshah*, 'a broom made of straw', (Gīl, 213).

Qasqas, 'to break', 'to cut into pieces', (Cha, *Ath*, 73).

Qaṭqaṭ, 'to become like small particles of frost', *qaṭ*, 'a small piece', CA; 'to curdle' (milk, yogurt), (Bak , 390; Cha, *Ath*, 73); 'to sharpen' (pencil), (Mac, II, 480; Wood, 375).

Ra'ra', ('Awwād, 23), 'to come into the prime of life' < *ru'ru'*, 'in full bloom', (Wehr, 345).

Rabrab, 'to complain vociferously', 'to raise hell', (Wood, 179); 'to use God's name (*rabb*) in vain when cursing and swearing' (Mac, I, 418), 'to talk a lot', 'to show one's anger like s.o. who often uses the word *rabb* (God)', (Sām, 199), Syr. 'same'. A few Iraqis say *rabrab il-'ajīn*, 'the dough fermented and rose'.

Raçraç, *rajraj*, 'to become weak, loose', 'to convulse, quiver' < *rajj* (Wood, 181).

Raḍraḍ, 'to bruise', (Mac, I, 418; Dabb, 141), 'to smash' (a bone), (al-Karmilī, (*Majmū'ah*, I, 129, n. 57; 304, n. 1) < *raḍḍ*, 'to bruise', (Wood, 189; Ḥana, *Mu'jam*, III, 190), *traḍraḍ*, 'to become bruised', (Mac, I, 434).

Rafraf, 'to flap the wings', (Wood, 191; Mac, I, 425), *raffa*, 'to twitch' (eyelid), Arm, *méraprōpéh*, 'to blink', (YM I, *Hebrew-Aramaic*, 301; Mac, I, 423), 'to flutter', (Erwin, *A Short Reference*, 78).

Rajraj 'to shake', 'to quiver' < *rajja*, 'to shake', (Wood, 181).

Rakhrakh, 'to soften a little by wetting' (clothes), *rakhkha* CA, 'to become soft', Syr, *rakhīkhā*, 'soft', 'wet' (clothes), (Bak, 233).

Ramram, ('Awwād, 23), 'to rot', 'to decay' < *rimma*, 'rot', 'decay', CA.

Raqraq, 'to dilute', 'to soften a lot', 'to have pity', (Wood, 192) < *raqqa*, 'to be minced or soft'.

Rashrash, 'to rustle'< *rashsha*, 'to make a jingling noise', 'to sprinkle around', 'to spray', (Wood, 188); 'to dazzle'; (DH, *Qāmūs*, 36), Syr, *rash*, CA, *rashsha*.

Raṣraṣ, 'to fill with melted lead', (Wood, 187), 'to join s.th. with lead' < *raṣāṣ*, 'lead' or < *raṣṣa*, 'to consolidate (a wall) by putting lead between the stones', 'to become solid, hard' (ground) < Syr, *raṣ*, *mraṣaṣ*, 'strong like lead', used figuratively about a strong person, (Sām, 199).

Raṭraṭ, 'to dirty a dress with mud', (Bak, 234; Ḥana, *Mu'jam*, III, 191) < *raṭiṭ*, 'soft mud'; 'to shiver', 'to shake',√ RWṬ or √ RṬṬ.

Ṣabṣab, 'to pour forth', 'to empty'< *ṣabba*, 'to pour', 'to cast', (Wood, 256); 'to shed tears', (al-Karmilī, *Majmū'ah*, I, 79, n. 2).

Ṣufṣuf, 'to set in a line or a row', 'to arrange'< *ṣaffa*, 'to align', (al-Karmilī, *Majmū'ah*, II, 217, n. 67),√ ṢFF.

Saksak < 'to grind one's teeth', (Gīl, 115), Heb, *siksék*, 'same'.

Salsal, 'to put in order', (Wood, 222), *silsilah*, 'a chain', 'to cause to flow' (tears) < Syr, 'same', (al-Karmilī, *Majmū'ah*, I, 129).

Rashrash, 'to scatter', (DH, *Qāmūs*, 152), 'to spray' < *rashrash* (the radicals are reversed), (*Muḥīṭ*, 460).

Samsam, 'to poison', 'to incite', (YD, *Sefat*, 167; Gīl, 117) < *summ*, 'poison', CA, *tsamsam*! 'eat!', said angrily wishing that the food becomes like a poison to the person who eats it, (Gīl, 133).

Sarsar, 'to fool around', (Gīl, 113); 'to act like a *serseri*' (Tur, 'rascal', 'bum'), (Mac, I, 418; Dul, 124; Thin, 52; YD, *Sefat*, 124), in Aramaic, 'one who behaves badly'.

Ṣarṣar, *ṣaghṣagh*, 'to make a sound like a cricket (*ṣurṣūr*)', (Bak, 308); 'to keep a lot of money in a *ṣurrah* (a purse or piece of cloth)'; 'to hum', 'to ring', (Sām, 199; Ḥana, *al-Alfāẓ*, 216), *ṣarra*, CA, 'to tie'.

Ṣawṣaw, *ṣōṣā* and *çōçā*, 'to chirp', (Ḥana, *Mu'jam*, I, 311) √ ṢWY. Baghdadi Jews use it also to mean 'to cast eyes on girls', (Gīl, 139).

Sha'sha', 'to shine', 'to dilute', CA (Bak, 150), *tsha'sha'*, 'to glitter', (al-Karmilī, *Majmū'ah*, II, 214, n. 10); 'to entertain', 'to delight', (Thin, 57), Heb, *shi'shé'a'*, 'same'; *tsha'sha'* 'to be melancholic', (Shāl, III, 78).

Shadshad, 'to tie tightly', (Mac, I, 425), *shadda*, CA, 'to tie', (Altoma, 59; Sām, 198).

Shagshag, *shaqshaq*, 'to rip', (Mac, I, 418; II, 519), *tshagshag*, 'to be cut into pieces', (Mac, I, 431; Wood, 245), 'to be unstitched and hang down', (YD, *Sefat*, 142).

Shakhshakh, 'to urinate while standing or walking < *shakhkha*, 'to urinate', CA (Bak, 284) as in *imm il-'ghōṣ min ferḥeta timshī wu-tshakhshik*, 'out of joy the bride's mother walks and urinates', (Ghulamī, 21).

Shakshak, 'to sting', *shakka*, 'to pierce', CA; 'to suspect', (YM II, *Aramaic-Kurdish*, 170); 'to thread', (Bak. 292).

Shalṭagh, 'cheat', (Wood, 247).

Shalbah, more commonly *tshalbah*, 'to climb up', (Wood, 247).

Shamsham, 'to sniff' < *shamma*, 'to smell', (Mac, I, 415; DH, *Qāmūs*, 157; YM I, *Hebrew-Aramaic*, 274), 'to spy' (fig.), (Gīl, 128; YD, *Sefat*, 196), *mashmōshéh*, 'to touch in order to feel s.th.', (YM II, *Aramaic-Kurdish*, 303).

Shanshal, 'to dangle', 'to lower', 'to spill', CA, 'to become loose', (DH, *Qāmūs*, 154), Heb, *shilshél*, 'to hang down'; < *nashala*, 'same', CA.

Sharshar < *sharra*, 'to drip'; 'to fall or spout like water', (DH, *Qāmūs*, 152), 'to dry clothes in the sun', (Gīl, 125; Sām,198), 'to scatter' (ashes), (DH, *Qāmūs*, 152); 'to spray' > *rashrash* (radicals are reversed, Bak, 460).

Ṭa'ṭa', 'to become weak', (Bak, 123); 'to abate' (heat), (Ḥana, *al-Alfāẓ*, 120); 'to perish', (Ghanīmah, 271), √ 'W; *mṭa'ṭa'*, 'incompetent', 'an incapable and unstable person', (Bak, 465).

Ta'ta', 'to walk' < *tātī*, said of a child who begins to take a step; 'to hesitate in speech', CA, (al-Munjid, 61[80]).

Ṭabṭab, 'to pat with the hands', (DH, *Qāmūs*, 178; Gīl, 15; Mac, II, 438; Bak, 318; Ḥajj, V, 359; VI, 105), *ṭabb*, 'to pat lightly', (Wood, 285).

Taftaf, 'to steal', 'to abduct'; 'to cough and spit', 'to say *tfī* or *tuff* (insulting expressions). In children's speech, *'énah tuffah*, means 'his eye is swollen', (Ḥana, *Mu'jam*, 81).

Ṭafṭaf, 'to drip from the side of a container' or when the edge of a garment touches the ground and makes a noise when walking, (Bak, 324).

Taḥtaḥ, (intr.) 'to move', ('Ubaydī, 48).

Taltal = *tantal*, 'to heap', 'to fill to the top', (Ḥana, *Mu'jam*, II, 120).

Ṭalṭal, 'to coat', CA, √ ṬLY.

Ṭamṭam, ('Awwād, 24), 'to hide' (tr.); 'to bury'; 'to cover up', (Ḥana, *Mu'jam*, II, 108) < *ṭamma*, CA, (Wood, 294), 'to bury'.

Ṭanṭan, 'to hum', 'to buzz' (flies), (Thin, 77; Turj, 73; Ḥajj, *al-Amthāl*, 278; Erwin, *A Short Reference*, 79) < *ṭanna*, CA, 'same'.

Taptap, 'to simmer' < Arm, *taptap*, (Cha, *Ath*, 64), 'to sizzle'.

Ṭaqṭaq, *ṭagṭag*, 'to make a cracking, popping noise' (roasting seeds), 'to crack repeatedly', (Gīl, 155; Erwin, *A Short Reference*, 79), < *ṭaqqa*, CA, 'to explode', 'to burst', (Wood, 291); 'to throb' (heart); (Ḥajj, IV, 274; V, 360). The following proverb is from the Euphrates villages: *ḥalgah yiṭagṭig'*, 'his throat is throbbing [for food]', (Shūḥān, 221[81]), an epithet said about a poor person, Arm, *méṭaqṭōqéh*, 'to pop', (YM I, *Hebrew-Aramaic* 249, II, 493); (YM II, *Aramaic-Kurdish*, 183; 'to lock repeatedly' [on a door]).

Ṭarṭar, 'to boast', 'to talk rubbish', (Gīl, 152) < *ṭarṭūr*, 'boaster', (Wood, 288), 'an epithet for one who breaks wind a lot', (Cha, *Ath*, 63; Ghanīmah, 271), 'to break dawn' < *ṭarra*, (Mac, II, 528).

Ṭashṭash, 'to throw here and there' < *ṭashsh*, 'to scatter', 'to disperse', (Wood, 289; Qad, I, 264); 'to become wet and soft after being soaked in liquid', *tashsha*, CA, 'same'.

Tastas, 'to pull back while facing forward' (tr.), (Bak, 113).

Ṭawṭaw, 'to blow the *ṭiwwāṭah*' (IA, 'trumpet'), 'to shout very loudly', (Gīl,157; YD, *Sefat*, 114; Thin, 52).

80 Al-Munjid, *al-Munjid fī al-Lughah* (Beirut 1998), (henceforth al-Munjid).

81 Aḥmad Shūḥān, *al-Amthāl al-Furātiyyāh* (Damascus 1984), (henceforth Shūḥān),

Wa'wa', ('Awwād, 25), 'to become aware', 'to pay attention', (Wood, 498), √ W'Y.

Wa'wa', 'to mumble', CA, 'to repeat the sound *wa*''.

Waçwaç, 'to chirp', 'to make the sound *waç, waç* a lot' (bird), (Thin, 263).

Wadhwadh, 'to be penniless', (Ḥana, *al-Alfāẓ*, 388).

Wahwah, ('Awwād, 25), 'to hesitate'; 'to be undecided and confused', (Ḥana, *Mu'jam*, II, 139).

Wajwaj, 'to blaze' < *ajja*, CA, 'same'; 'to appear as a vivid colour', (Bak, 492).

Wakhwakh, CA, 'to intend', 'to have in mind', *wakhā*, 'same', √ WKhY.

Walwal, ('Awwād, 25), 'to cry *yā wayla*', 'to wail repeatedly', 'to moan', CA.

Wanwan, 'to moan repeatedly', (Wood, 504), 'to groan', (Mac, I, 418) < *anna*, CA, 'to moan a lot', 'to complain', *anna*, 'same', CA, (Gīl, 15; YD, *Sefat*, 161).

Waqwaq, 'to cuckoo', 'to make the sound *waq waq*', 'to croak', 'to long for' (fig.); ('Awwād, 25; Gīl, 281; YD, *Sefat*, 216).

Warwar, 'to blaze', (Mac, I, 415; Ghanīmah, 270; Bak, 492), by extension 'to be furious', (Thin, 264), Arm, *warwārā*, 'a spark of fire', (Cha, *Ath*, 87) < *warra*, CA, 'to blaze'.

Waswas, 'to be apprehensive', (Wood, 494; Gīl, 278; Mac, I, 418; YD, *Sefat*, 215), CA, 'same', (Wright, I, 47).

Waṣwaṣ, 'to twitter', 'to chirp', (YD, *Sefat*, 215).

Waṭwaṭ, ('Awwād, 25), 'to blow a trumpet' < *waṭwāṭ*, 'trumpet'.

Watwat, ('Awwād, 25), 'to stutter', (Gīl, 276); 'to complain to o.s.', (YD, *Sefat*, 206).

Wazwaz, 'to buzz' < *azza*, CA, (DH, *Qāmūs*, 300); 'to hum', 'to twitter', (Piamenta, II, 522; Gīl, 277; YD, *Sefat*, 272; Bak, 495), < *wazza* 'to make a sound like a goose' (*wiz wiz*), 'to waddle'; 'to be enraged', (Thin, 266).

Zabzab, 'to bundle securely', 'to tie with a rope' < *zabba*, 'to gather', 'to be firm', 'to leak', CA, (Turj, 121).

Zafzaf, 'to scold', *zaff*, (Wood, 204), Heb, *nazaf*, 'same'.

Zaghzagh, 'to tickle', (DH, *Qāmūs*, 131).

Zaḥzaḥ, 'to move out' (tr.), 'to displace', (YD, *Sefat*, 217; Wood, 201; Sām, 198) > *itzaḥzaḥ*, or *izzaḥzaḥ*, 'to move a little', (Wood, 201).

Zakzak, 'to tickle', 'to touch lightly' < *zakka*, 'same', (*Muḥīṭ*, 375).

Zamzam, 'to challenge and be haughty', (Bak, 249). In Mosul, they say *zamzam bil-jīgārah*, 'he boasted smoking a cigarette', (Bak, 249). In CA, 'to rumble'.

Zanzan, 'to indulge in fornication' √ ZNY, *tzanzan*, 'to behave like a woman' < Per, *zan*, 'woman', (Cha, *Kalimāt*, 40).

Zaqzaq, 'to chirp', 'to peep', (Wood, 204). In Mosul they say *zaqzaqit 'i'ṣéfīgh baṭnī*, 'I was hungry' (lit. 'the sparrows of my belly grumbled', [Bak, 384]).

Zarzar, 'to move the pupils', *tzarzar*, an epithet, 'to be anxious, annoyed', (Ḥajj, *al-Amthāl*, 222). Some Iraqis say *tlazliz* instead (Ḥana, *Mu'jam*, III, 241); CA, 'to chirp'.

Zatzat, ('Awwād, 24), 'to send away', *zatt*, (tr.), 'to move quickly' (intr.), (Wood, 201); 'to throw', (Bak, 238); < *zattat*, 'to direct and guide somebody to the road', (CA) < dissim. *zattat* > dissim. *zatzat*,*-tt* >*tz*.

Wahwas, ('Awwād, 25), 'to worry and feel uneasy' < *hawwas*, (Wood, 505), dissim. *ww* >*hw*.

APPENDIX II

Type 1.2. 1.4

Ba'baṣ, 'to feel s.th. with one's finger' (*'iṣba'*), a shifting of letters occurred in the stem √ ṢB' > √ B'Ṣ, then *ba'aṣ* > *ba'baṣ*, 'to poke', (Wood, 38; Shal, I, 363; Sām, 153). This verb is employed in the epithets *yiba'biṣ iblīṣ*, 'he pokes the devil', (Ḥajj, *al-Amthāl*, 323), and *yiba'biṣ il-sabi'*, 'he pokes the lion', said about a person who causes harm and trouble to himself, (Ḥana, *Mu'jam*, I, 544). Likewise, *ba'baṣ il-ḥkiyyī*, 'he spoiled the matter', hence, 'he complicated matters', (YD, *Sefat*, 158), and about unlucky person the phrase *ḥaẓẓ mba'baṣ* is employed, (Shāl, I, 587). A person who does evil is poked by the devil: *ba'baṣ ah il-shīṭān*, (Shāl, I, 363).

Barbag, *barbaq*, *baghbaq*, 'to bubble' (water from the drain, sink, etc.), (Ḥana, *Mu'jam*, I, 48), 'to squirt', 'to spray'; Arm, *mébarbōqéh*, (YM I, *Hebrew-Aramaic*, 132; Soko, 241) or < *baghbūghtā*, Arm, 'a bubble on the water' or 'a blister on the skin', (Cha, *Ath*, 21); 'to complain angrily', (fig, Gīl, 23); 'to shine', 'to glitter', (Piamenta, I, 28).

Barbaṣ, 'to irrigate the land', Arm, *rbaṣ*, 'same', (Ch, *Ath*, 46), or *barrasa*, 'to water', dissim. *-bb-* > *-rb-*.

Barbaṭ, 'to intertwine' (thread), (Ḥana, *Mu'jam*, I, 487); 'to rip off', CA; *mébarbōṭéh*, Arm, 'to flap', (YM I, *Hebrew-Aramaic*, 218), Syr, *frāṭ*, 'same'.

Balbaz, 'to look carefully while the pupils are shining' < *ballaza*, dissim. *-ll-* > *-lb-* (Ḥana, *Mu'jam*, I, 584).

Barba', 'to flourish and be satisfied' < *rabī'*, 'spring', or *raba'a* (Sām, 193); 'to thrive', 'to prosper', (MM, 61; Shal, III, 9; Tikritī V, 100[82]); 'to scare', (Ḥana, *Mu'jam*, I, 487; Gīl, 27; Bak, 75; Mac, I, 421); 'to soak', as in *barbi' il-khubzah bil-ḥalīb*, 'soak the piece of bread in the milk', (Wood, 30); *mébarbō'é*, 'to scare', used by Baghdadi Jews); (YM I, *Hebrew-Aramaic*, 218), *itbarba'*, 'to become afraid and confused', Arm, *ithparpa'*, (Cha, *Ath*, 24).

Barbad, 'to destroy', 'break off', (Sām, 153), Per, *barbād*, 'destruction', (Ḥajj, *al-Amthāl*, 39); 'to be left with nothing following a calamity', (Shal, I, 318).

Barbaj, *barbakh*, 'to sit and relax', (Sām, 153, 193), *rabakha*, CA, 'same'.

---

82 'Abd al-Raḥmān al-Tikrītī, *Jamharat al-Amthāl al-Baghdādiyyah* (Baghdad 1986), V, (henceforth Tikritī V).

Dahdar/gh, 'to roll along', 'to cause to roll' < *hadara*, (Mac, I, 432; Piamenta, I, 144); 'to send', as in *dahdirha-l-'Alī, tara dīqah*, 'send ʿAlī to him, be aware that he's his friend'; 'to let out' (remark), as in *dahdarha lil-iḥçāya giddām in-nās*, (Wood, 167).

Dahwar, (ʿAwwād, 23), 'roll along', (Piamenta, I, 144; Wood, 168), √ HWR, 'to hurl down'; 'to topple', *iddahwar*, 'to tumble, roll', (Bak, 230), 'to go along', as in *rūḥ iddahdar (itdahwar) ghiddāmna w-ba'dén iḥna nijī warāk*, 'go along in front of us, and afterwards we shall come behind you', (Mac, I, 432).

Dahraj and *dahrab* (ʿAwwād, 23), 'to roll down' (tr.), CA, 'same', < *daraj*, 'stare'.

Dalham, 'to be dark, gloomy' < *dalham*, 'very dark', 'gloomy'.*Dandal*, 'to hang down', (Mac, I, 432), 'to lower s.th. from above', (DH, *Qāmūs*, 111; Ḥajj, I, 425; IV, 268; Wood, 166; Gīl, 93; Cha. *Ath*, 44), Arm, *médandōléh*, 'to lower', (YM II, *Aramaic-Kurdish*, 228; Bak, 226), < *dandal*, CA, 'same', 'to hang down', 'to bring to the ground', (Mac, I, 416).

Daqdas, 'to search', 'to make holes', (DH, *Qāmūs*, 109).

Darda', 'to curse, making a gesture with a finger denoting intercourse', used by some Iraqi and Kuwaiti women. This gesture is called in Kuwait, *dardū'ah*, (Ḥana, *al-Alfāẓ*, 130).

Dardaḥ, *mdardaḥ*, 'expert', 'experienced', (DH, *Qāmūs*, 261).

Dardaq, 'to produce a sound when pouring water from a jar' < *darraqa*, CA, 'to pour water', (Bak, 219; Sām, 193; ʿUbaydī, 48), or dissim. *-rr-* > *-rd-*, 'to walk quickly', 'to raise' (a child), Arm, (Soko, 262). The Hebrew verb *dirdéq* means 'to teach children' < *dardāq*, Arm, 'a child', *déqaqa*, 'a tender child'; (Cha, *Ath*, 41), *daqīq*, 'delicate', 'tiny', CA.

Dardash, 'to chat a lot', 'to talk nonsense', (Ḥana, *Mu'jam*, III, 45; Sām, 160), 'to deliver a sermon', Arm, *dérasha*, 'sermon'; in the Talmud, 'to argue', 'to debate', 'to complain', (fig., Gīl, 90).

Dardam, 'to mumble', (Wood, 156); 'to mutter to o.s. angrily', (Shāl, II, 31) < *damdamah*, 'anger', CA; dard *mand*, Per, 'being in pain', (Ḥana, *Mu'jam*, III, 45; Mac, II, 524).

Farfaḥ, 'to become happy' < *fariḥa*, 'to become cheerful', (TA, 51), *tfarfaḥ*, 'to throb out of happiness', Arm, *farfiḥīnā*, 'to flap wings while on the ground', (Thin, 111). Some Iraqis say, *farfaḥat rūḥah*, 'he was embarrassed and confused', (Thin, 111, n. 30; Sām, 173). Baghdadi Jews use this verb to mean 'to be at one's last gasp', (Gīl, 96).

Farfaṭ, *faghfaṭ*, 'to sop' (bread) < *farraṭa*, dissim. *-rr-* > *-rf-*, 'to scatter' (grapes), (Bak, 367; Ḥana, *al-Alfāẓ*, 277); 'to crumble', 'to break open a pomegranate', < *farrṭa* or Arm, *parpaṭ*, (Cha, *Ath*, 68); 'to take the seeds out', (Wood, 349; Gīl, 200).

Fa'faṣ, 'to crumple', 'to irritate' < or *fi'aṣ*, 'to dent', (Wood, 357).

Falfaṣ, 'to twist and pull o.s. in order to be free'; (Thin, 116; Bak, 369); 'to try'.

Falgaḥ, more commonly *tfalgaḥ*, 'to turn one's back laughing when lying down or sitting', (Thin, 117).

Falsaf, 'to check s.th. in a philosophizing way', (Thin, 116). to move' (intr.), (Sām, 175).

Qarqa', 'to become worn out', 'to make noise continuously', (Gīl, 250; Ben-Jacob, *Hebrew and Aramaic*, 180; Mac, I, 416), 'to squeak', (Ḥana, II, *Mu'jam*, 99) < *gargū'ah*, 'weak', (al-Karmilī, *Majmū'ah*, II, 153); 'to thunder', (Wood, 388); 'to rock', (Thin, 163), *tgarga'* (an epithet), 'to be frightened', (Ḥana, *Mu'jam*, II, 99).

Gargam, 'to thunder', as in *gargemit il-dinī*, 'it was thundering', (Gīl, 59), *mégargoméh* (YM I, *Hebrew-Aramaic*, 225), *mgargam*, 'under developed child', (Thin, 163).

Gargaṣ, 'to squat', (Wood, 388).

Gōgā < *jōjā*, 'to hum' (child), (Ghanīmah, 267).

Janjal, 'to make a loud voice', 'to toll', (Ḥana, *Mu'jam*, II, 238; Bak, 147; Gīl, 54), < CA, *juljul*, 'a small bell'.

Jōjal, 'to rotate or shake wheat, rice, etc. in a sieve or tray', i.e. 'to polish grains so that the pebbles and dust settle in the bottom' < Arm, *jōjālā*, 'going around', 'moving food in the mouth', (DH, *Qāmūs*, 81; Bak, 149); (Cha, *Ath*, 32; DH, *Qāmūs*, 81; Bak, 149); CA, *jawjala*, *ajāla*.

Ka'kal, 'to make a hairlock' < *ka'kūlah* < 'the crest of a bird', 'a hairlock', (Wood, 407); 'to become wrinkled' (hair), (Bak, 414), *tka'kal*, 'to become kinky', (Mac, I, 432).

Kankar, (Basra), 'to become curly' (hair), 'to put on an *'iqāl'*, (a round headgear), (Thin, 152; Baz, 147), *kankarah*, Per, 'top of everything', (Thin, 152), *mkankar*, 'curly'.

Karkash, 'to sew on a *karkūshah*' (tassel), (Sām, 179); 'to sew a strip on the hem of a dress' (YD, *Sefat*, 142; al-Karmilī, *Majmū'ah*, II, 219, n. 17; Wood, 222; Gīl, 226) < *karkasha*, Arm, 'a wide belt made of wool', (Cha, *Ath*, 75).

Karkat, (or *karrakat*), 'to settle on an egg in order to hatch it' (hen), (Baghdad), (Ḥana, *al-Alfaẓ*, 155).

Kamkash, 'to grope', 'to feel one's way with the fingers' (in the dark), (Erwin, *A Short Reference*, 79; Thin, 151); 'to tuck s.th. in a shirt', (Sām, 193) < Per, *kamkasht*, (Baz, 151); 'to break' (dawn), Arm, (Cha, *Ath*, 32).

Kaskan, 'to become irritated', 'to have a hot temper', (Wood, 405) < Tur, *keskin*, 'tart', 'piquant', 'pungent'.

Laghlab, 'to join two pieces of fabric with a needle or pin', (Bak, 441).

Lahlab, 'to set on fire', (Sām, 193; Thin, 201), 'to become very hot', (Gīl, 239; YD, *Sefat*, 46) < *lahiba*, CA or < *luhba*; Arm, *malhōbéh*, 'to stoke a fire', (YM I, *Hebrew-Aramaic*, 261).

Lahlaj, 'to curdle' (milk), (Thin, 201).

Lōla, 'to sing a lullaby', (Thin, 200; Erwin, *A Short Reference*, 79; Wood, 430).

Lōlab, 'to screw' (a nut) < *lawlab*, 'a screw'.

Lōlaḥ, 'to hang s.th', (Thin, 199), more commonly *tlōlaḥ*, 'to wobble while walking', (Thin 153; Gīl, 39)

Ma'mas, ('Awwād, 25), 'to rub strongly' (leather), < *ma'asa*, 'to rub', or *'ammasa*, 'to crush s.th.', dissim. *-mm-* > *-'m*.

Maḥmaṣ, *tmaḥmaṣ*, 'to envy', (Gīl, 42; YD, *Sefat*, 128).

Marmad, 'to hide s.th.', 'to kill a man without leaving a clue', (Thin, 211).

Marmag, *tmarmag*, 'to become soft', *murmūgah*, 'soft' (watermelon, cantaloupe, etc.), (Thin, 211).

Marmagh, 'to sully', (DH, *Qāmūs*, 263) < *marragha*, CA, 'to roll in dust', dissim. *rr* > *rm*, 'to massage', 'to anoint' < *marakha*, CA, and Heb, *maraḥ*, 'same'; 'to become soft' (gland), (Thin, 211).

Marmaṣ, 'to eat with a hearty appetite' < *mariṣa*, CA; 'to point a finger or play with the breast' (baby), (Sām, 194; Thin, 211).

Marmaṭ, ('Awwād, 25), 'to pluck leaves off a branch forcefully' < *mariṭa*, or *marraṭa*, (Sām, 194), Heb, *maraṭ*, 'same', and figuratively, 'to torment', Syr (FM, 522); 'to tarry', 'to put off', (Thin, 211).

Na'nash, 'to rejuvenate', 'to be invigorated'< *nashsha* > *na'nash*.

Naghnaf, ('Awwād, 25), 'to eat s.th. with worms' < *naghf*, 'worm'.

Na'nas, 'to doze', 'to lull' < *na'isa*, 'to be sleepy and languid', (Sām, 194).

Qahqar < *qahira*, CA, 'to humiliate', 'to cause pain', (DH, *Qāmūs*, 228), *tqahqar*, 'to suffer'.

Qarqad, 'to become dry' (bread) < CA, *qarida*, 'same', (DH, *Qāmūs*, 222, *Muḥīṭ*, 730), (AF, *Mu'jam*, 138), 'same'.

Qarqaj, 'to shout', 'to complain', 'to speak loudly', (YD, *Sefat*, 158) < *qaraj*, 'loud', Per, 'chatter box', (Gīl, 212).

Qarqaṣ, *gargaṣ*, 'to squat on one's heels', (DH, *Qāmūs*, 222); 'to gnaw', 'to munch', (Wood, 388).

Qarqash, 'to chew', 'to gnaw', (Wood, 388; DH, *Qāmūs*, 222), 'to make noise when eating crispy food or walking on dry leaves'< Arm, *qarqashtā*, 'noise of thunder', (Cha, *Ath*, 70; Ḥajj, *al-Amthāl*, 266, n. 9) < *qarasha* or *qarrasha*, 'to cut in circles', dissim. *-rr-* > *rsh-* (Gīl, 212; YD, *Sefat*, 43; Bak, 369), 'to gnaw'.

Ṣamṣagh, 'to save money in a bag' (Christians in Mosul), < *ṣarrā*, 'same'. The Baghdadis say *ṣammad* (Wood, 269).

Ṣanṣal, 'to drip' (vessel, bottle), Arm, *ménaṣōléh*, (YM I, *Hebrew-Aramaic*, 290; YD, *Sefat*, 133); 'to pour', (Kāmil, 76). The Baghdadi Jews say *naṣṣal*, 'to leak a little', (Bak, 311).

Sansal, 'to link together', (Ḥajj, *al-Amthāl*, 292, n. 72; Wood, 222), *silsilah*, 'chain'.

Sarbas, 'to float on water'. (Sām, 165) < *saraba*.

Sarsab, *saghsab*, 'to flow', 'to infiltrate' < *saraba*, ('Ubaydī, 48); 'to walk slowly', (Bak, 120); 'to cause to sink', (Shīr, 90); 'to cause to float', (Sām, 165).

Saḥsal, 'to drag forcefully', (Wood, 214), 'to do a job slowly', (Gīl, 112) < *saḥala*, 'to drag', 'to be slow', (Bak, 262), *msaḥsal'*, 'a long dress that touches the ground', or 'a slow person', (Ḥajj, VI, 135).

Shaḥshaṭ, 'to scuff', 'to scrape', < *shiḥaṭ*, IA, 'to drag along', (Wood, 236); 'to pull', 'Ubaydī, 49); 'to have barely enough' or 'to become scarce' < *shaḥḥaṭ*, 'to economize', (Bak, 463).

Shalshal, 'to drip' (water, blood).

Shanshal, < *shalshal*. In the Syrian dialect there is an expression, *il-shajara mshanshilī*, 'the tree is loaded with fruits and the fruits are attached to each other like dangling chains', (FM, 305). The change of the first *l* > *n* is to facilitate the pronunciation of the two *lāms* in the verb *shalshal*, 'to become tired' (informal); 'to lower', 'to spill', CA, 'to become loose', (DH, *Qāmūs*, 154), Heb, *shilshél*, 'to hang down'.

Sarsaḥ, 'to comb hair smoothly', 'to hang down' (hair), (YD, *Sefat*, 143); 'to shed tears', (al-Karmilī, *Majmū'ah*, I, 272, n. 3).

Sharshab, *shaghshab*, 'to hang down' (a loose thread from a dress), (Gīl, 125; YD, *Sefat*, 142).

Sharshaḥ < *sharraḥ*, 'to slice', 'to unravel' (string), 'to become loose, weak' and figuratively, 'to humiliate, disgrace', (DH, *Qāmūs*, 153; Bak, 85), dissim. *-rr-* > *-rsh-*.

Sharshakh, 'to be unstitched and dangle' (a loose thread from a dress), (Gīl, 123; YD, *Sefat*, 142).

Shōshaṭ, 'to burn' (food), √ ShWṬ; 'to scorch', 'to become upset or disturbed', (Wood, 253).

Ṭarṭab, 'to be soaked' (clothes), < *raṭṭaba*, 'to wet', (Thin, 73; Sām, 170).

Tarṭaḥ, 'to be in rage' (fig.), Syr, *rṭaḥ*, Heb, *rataḥ*, 'to boil'.

Wahwan, ('Awwād, 25), 'to be weak', *waḥana*, 'same'.

Wahwas, 'to hesitate', 'to be doubtful', (Wood, 505).

Zōzā, 'to become very hot', 'to move a lot' (ants), Kur, 'same', (Bak, 254).

APPENDIX III

Denominatives:

'Ad'ad, 'to moan' < *'addadah*, IA, 'a professional moaner', Arm, *mé'ad'ōdéh*, 'to moan', (YM I, *Hebrew-Aramaic*, 276).

'Aḍraṭ, more commonly *t'aḍraṭ*, 'to become out of order' (slang), (Thin, 90); *zeraṭa*, Tur, *zarta*, 'breaking wind'.

Aflas, 'to be bankrupt' < *fils*, 'the smallest value of currency in Iraq', (Bak, 369).

'Afrat, 'to be a bully', 'to act tough', (Wood, 314).

'Aftar, 'to take by force'; (Gīl, 172; Thin, 92) < *'aftarah*, 'chaos', 'disorder', *t'aftar 'alā*, 'to behave cruelly towards', 'to embezzle', (Ḥana, *Mu'jam*, II, 77). It is possible that *'afrat*, 'to behave like an *'ifrīt*' (a demon) > 'after'.

'Akmak, 'to become fat' < *'ukkah*, 'fat', (Thin, 94).

'Alqam, 'to embitter', 'to make suffer' < *'alqam*, 'a bitter plant', (Bak, 343).

'Anbalat, 'to act shamefully', 'to be lustful' (woman) < *'unbulah*, 'clitoris', (Thin, 96), Heb, *'inbāl*, 'clapper' (of a bell), *'uvula*' (vulg.).

'Anzagh, *'anzar*, 'to be stubborn and refuse to carry out an assignment', (Bak, 345).

'Armal, 'to roll in dust'< Arm, *'arpal*, 'same', (Cha, *Ath*, 66), *t'armal* < Arm, *ith'arpal*, 'to be rolled in dust'.

'Askar, 'to build a military base', 'to camp' < *'askar*, 'soldiers', (Sām, 190).

Adhnab, 'to sin', (Wood, 175) < *dhanab*, 'an offence, a sin'.

Arba', 'to spend the spring' < *rabī'*, 'spring', (al-Karmilī, *Majmū'ah*, I, 342, n. 4).

Aslam, 'to become a Muslim' < Muslim or < Islam.

Balbas, 'to make a devil of s.o.' < *iblīs*, 'devil', (Sām, 154).

Balshaf, 'to Bolshevize', *tbalshaf*, 'to be Bolshevized', (Wehr, 72).

Bashnaq, ('Awwād, 22), more commonly *tbashnaq*, 'to put on a *pashnūqah*' (a head cover), Arm, *pashnūghah*, (Cha, *Ath*, 30; Shīr, 17).

Baghnak, *tbaghnak*, 'to sit like an important person', (Bak, 452).

Barghal, 'to live in a village or a land close to a source of water', (Cha, *Kalimāt*, 16, 36).

Balwar, 'to crystallize', *ballūr*, 'fine glass', 'crystal', 'rock crystal', (Bak, 91), Tur, *ballūr*.

Bastan, 'to go to a park for pleasure', (Bak, 112), Per, *bustān*, 'orchard'.

Basṭan, 'to sit on the floor with legs crossed', (Bak, 452).

Bōbaj, 'to hit the face or the head with *bābūj* < Tur, *babuç*, 'a wooden slipper'.

Ça'waç, 'to turn upside down and subdue s.o. in order to beat his/her feet' (tr.), (Ḥana, *Mu'jam*, II, 293). It is likely that *ka'akka*, CA, 'to cause s.o. or s.th. to look like a doughnut', and figuratively 'to cause pain and torture'.

Çarçaf, 'to cover with a bed sheet' < Tur, *çarçaf*, 'bed sheet', (MM, 126; Wood, 84; Sām, *al-Dakhīl*, 71; TA, 40; Shīr, 99).

Çarkaz, 'to become Circassian', (Ḥana, *Fiqh*, 63).

Çéwar, 'to turn around', (Thin, 65; Ḥana, *al-Alfāẓ*, 89; MM, 133; Baz, 65; Mac, II, 414); 'to toss s.o. to the ground and beat his/her feet with a stick', (Ḥana, *Mu'jam*, II, 318); 'to beat up', (Erwin, *A Short Reference*, 79).

Daghbas, *darbas*, 'to bow one's head in silence while walking in the road' < *darb*, 'road', (Bak, 220); CA, 'to bolt' (a door), < *dirbās*, 'a bolt'; *mdarbas*, (DH, *Qāmūs*, 261).

Dalgham, 'to be angry', (Ḥana, *Mu'jam*, III, 62); 'to look gloomy', (Sām, 161; Bak, 224; Gīl, 91; Wood, 163) < *daghm*, CA, 'darkness'; 'to shape s.th. like a ball and roll it', *damlaq*, CA, 'same'.

Dambal, 'to break out in pimples', *mdanbal* (*m* > *n*), 'having an abscess' < *dimbilah*, 'a pimple', (Wood, 164; Mac, I, 216).

Darbā, 'to roll, cause to roll', 'to drift', as in *lammā māḥṣṣal flūs min abūh iddarbā 'alayya*, 'when he did not get money from his father, he drifted to me', (Wood, 155).

Darbas, 'to mould into a round shape' < *dabbas*, 'same', *mdarbas*, 'rounded-shape', (DH, *Qāmūs*, 261).

Darwaz, 'to beg'< Per, *darvāzéh*, 'the front of a house' where mendicants beg, referring to those who sit at the end of a road or at the threshold of a door begging', (Shīr, 62; Sām, *al-Dakhīl*, 53; Ḥana, *Mu'jam*, III, 49).

Darzan, 'to stitch', 'to moisten fabric before sewing', 'to sew with long loose stitches', *dariz*, 'basting', (Thin, 75).

Darwaj, 'to walk', 'to advance slowly' < *daraja*, 'step', 'stair'.

Dashlam, 'to suck a sugar cube in the mouth while sipping tea', (Bak, 219; MM, 155; Wood, 158; Ḥana, *Mu'jam*, III, 120); Tur, *dishlemek*, 'to nibble', 'to bite'.

Dastar, 'to mark a straight line on the wall by stretching a thread on it, in order to lay a straight row of bricks' (Sām, 188; Ḥana, *Mu'jam*, III, 53); 'to arrange something well', (Mac, I, 421); < Per, *dastār*, 'handkerchief, cloth'. In wrestling, *dastar mukhālaf* means 'to put one hand between the thighs of the opponent and the other hand on his hip and lift him from the floor', (Ḥana, *Mu'jam*, III, 53).

Déram, 'to put on *dayram'*, Per, 'green skin of the walnut tree' used as a cosmetic, (Ḥana, *al-Alfāẓ*, 141; al-Karmilī, *Dīwān*, 674).

Dharnaḥ, more commonly *tdharnaḥ*, 'to be annoyed', 'to feel revulsion', (Ḥana, *Mu'jam*, II, 45), < *dharnūḥ*, 'a type of insect', (Thin, 44, n. 3), said about a person who hates something, CA; 'to pretend weakness', (Sām, 162).

Dōdā, 'to crawl like a worm' < *dūd*, 'worms', (Sām, 188), 'to become seriously infected with worms', (Wood, 168).

Dōhan, 'to oil' < *dihin*, 'oil', or < *dāḥana*, 'same', (Sām, 188).

Dōhas, 'to imagine things due to *waswās*' (whispering of the devil or of the soul), 'to be neurotic', (Bak, 228); *madhūs*, (DH, *Qāmūs*, 261); 'to become lazy and tired', (Ḥana, *Mu'jam*, III, 111).

Dōḥas, 'to become seriously swollen or infected in the finger', (Wood, 168).

Ḍōjar, *tḍō jar*, 'to be annoyed', (Ḥana, *Mu'jam*, III, 73).

Dōkhan, 'to cause dizziness', (Gīl, 94; Ḥana, *Mu'jam*, II, 34; DY) √ DWKh, or *dakhkhana*, 'to smoke a cigarette', (Ḥana, *Mu'jam*, III, 97) √ DKhN.

Dōman, 'to win at dominoes', 'to end a game of dominoes', (YD, *Sefat*, 151; Ḥana, *Mu'jam*, III, 18; Erwin, *A Short Reference*, 79); 'to be in the habit of' < *dāman* (Wood, 165). In CA, 'to run away'; 'to be rotten and black' (palm tree), (Bak, 393); 'to fume', Tur, *dūmān*, 'smoke', 'fumes'.

Faghwaz, *parwaz*, ('Awwād, 22), 'to frame', (Ḥana, *Mu'jam*, I, 689; Gīl, 205), 'to sew a hem' < Per, *parwāz*, 'a hem' or 'the side of a frame', (Bak, 368).

Ga'naṣ, 'to emit a bad smell', *mga'naṣ*, 'bad', 'unripe' (fruits and vegetables) < Arm, *g'īṣā*, 'ugly', 'hated', (Cha, *Ath*, 84).

Gharbal, 'to sift', (Mac, I, 416), *gharbāl*, 'sieve'.

Ghōghā < Arm, *gāwgī*, 'to coo' (bird, baby), 'to speak tenderly to a child', (Ch, *Ath*, 67; Ghanīmah, 267).

Gōtar, 'to hurry away', (Ḥajj, *al-Amthāl*, 284, n. 88; Thin, 181; al-Karmilī, *Majmū'ah*, 305, I, n. 2).

Halyan, 'to become fresh and juicy like *halyūn* (asparagus)', (Shīr, 70).

Ḥarmal, 'to be unproductive' (tree) < *ḥarmūl*, as in *ḥarmalat il-rummānah*, 'the pomegranate did not ripen because of dryness', (Ḥana, *Mu'jam*, II, 358).

Ja'maṣ, 'to talk nonsense' or 'to use foul language' < *ja'mūṣ*, (vulg.) 'dry faeces', (Wood, 73; Bak, 143) < Syr, *j'āṣ* or *j'āz* (FM, 100); 'to be irritated', 'to shrink out of fear', (Gīl, 52; Ḥana, *Mu'jam*, II, 213; YD, *Sefat*, 159).

Jalfaṭ, 'to fill the gaps in a ship's deck' < *jalafa*, CA, 'same', 'to pronounce words unclearly making no sense' (fig.); 'to remove pieces of meat containing veins' < *julfūṭah*, 'inedible pieces of meat', (Sām, 155), or < *jalbaṭa*, 'to become sticky', the infix *b* of *jalbaṭa* > *f* > *jalafa*, 'to peel' (skin), 'to draw' (sword).

Jalham, 'to become very dark', (Ḥana, *Mu'jam*, II, 226) < *jahm*, CA, 'darkness', (Mac, II, 544).

Jalmad, < *jalmaṭ*, 'to shave the head with a razor' (the *m* is an infix), *jalaṭa*, CA, 'same', (Ḥana, *Mu'jam*, II, 225).

Jangar, 'to make a loud annoying noise', (Naqqāsh, *Nzūlah*, 115) < *jangūl*, 'the sound of metal or bells', (Ḥana, *Mu'jam*, II, 242; Thin, 35, n. 7). It is likely that this verb is based on *jangūl*, Per, 'sound of banging pieces of iron similar to that of a group of people talking in loud voices' < *jangar*, 'a group of people'

Jawrab, 'to dress s.o. in stockings', (Sām, 187).

Jōrab, 'to put on socks', *jūrāb*, 'stockings', (Shīr, 48), Per, *jūrāb* (TA, 22).

Ka'wak, 'to coil', 'to shape s.th. like a spiral', *tka'wak*, 'to coil o.s.' (snake), (Bak. 130, 414).

Kalbas, 'to clip', 'to staple', (Sām, 191) < *kalbaç*, 'to handcuff' < Tur, *kelepçe*, 'handcuffs'; Arm, *mékalmoçé* (YM I, *Hebrew-Aramaic*, 205).

Karmaz, 'to hit with a fist', Arm, *kurméz*, 'a fist'.

Karzal, 'to collect and arrange s.th, randomly', (Thin, 140), 'to become like *kirzillah*' an epithet for 'burden', lit, 'a heavy mass of stones', (Gīl, 339).

Khalqan, 'to become worn-out' (dress) < *khaliq*, 'shabby', (Ḥajj, IV, 135; Baz, 37).

Khanfas, 'to die out' (flame), 'to calm down', (Wood, 147; Ḥana, *al-Alfāẓ*, 120); 'to become black like a beetle' (*khunfusah*), (Bak, 200; Ḥana, *Mu'jam*, II, 535) < *khafasa*, 'to be silent and introvert', (Shāl, I, 349).

Kharkhash, 'to rattle', Per, *kharkhāsh*, 'poppy', (Wood, 132; Sām, 159; YD, *Sefat*, 234).

Kharshan, 'to become coarse' (surface) < *kharsh*, 'a scratch', (Bak, 196) or < IA, *khashin*, 'same'.

Khatyar, 'to become old' < *khityār* (Cha, *Ath*, 37).

Khélaq, 'to curse', (Cha, *Kalimāt*, 69), said as a wish or statement (Mosul) < *khlūqah*, 'a curse', (Bak, 198), as in *illī -y- khéliq il-nās yikhélqōnu wiy-ni'lōn 'ummu wabūnu*, 'he who curses people, he and his father will be cursed', (Bak, 202).

Khōṣar, *tkhōṣar*, 'to put one's hands on one's hips' < *khuṣr*, 'hip', (Sām, 188; Bak, 116; Ḥana, *Mu'jam*, II, 44).

Khōzaq, *qōzagh*, 'to impale', 'to embarrass', (Gīl, 83; YD, *Sefat*, 157), < *qāzūgh*, CA, 'same'; OTur, *qāzīq*, 'stick', 'stake', (Shāl, II, 394), or < *khazzaqa*, 'to become angry', dissim. *-zz-* > *-wz-* (Bak, 121; Sām, 165), or *khawzaqa*, CA, 'to get s.o. into a bad fix' (fig.), (Gīl, 83; al-Karmilī, *Majmū'ah*, I, 244, n. 6; Wood, 148) or <

khāzūq, 'a skewer', 'a stick', (Thin, 128; Cha, *Kalimāt*, 43; Shāl, I, 431); *tqōzagh*, 'to be in trouble' (fig.) (YD, *Sefat*, 157).

Khōshag, 'to stir (tea) with *khāshūgah*' (spoon), Per, *qāshuq*; OTur, *kashīk*, (Turj, 38; Ḥana, *Mu'jam*, II, 442).

Lastak, 'to tie'< *lastīk*', 'rubber wrapped with fabric to tie goods'.

Ma'ghal, 'to beat', (YD, *Sefat*, 167; Bak, 202).

Marjaḥ, 'to swing' (intr.), *tmarjaḥ*, 'to swing' (tr.), (Wood, 435; Sām, 181; Mac, I, 216), < *'urjūḥah*, CA.

Maṣghan, 'to cause pain' (fig.), 'to twist s.th. into the shape of a *miṣrān*' (intestine), (Ḥana, *Mu'jam*, II, 112), *tmaṣghan*, 'to be powerless and in pain', (YD, *Sefat*, 162).

Mashwar, 'to promenade' < *mishwār*, 'a short walk', (DH, *Qāmūs*, 267).

Mashyakh, 'to install a *shaykh* (sheik), a chief'.

Maskan, 'to settle s.o. in a shelter or home', 'to mortgage' < Arm, *mashkintah'*, 'mortgage', (YM I, *Hebrew-Aramaic*, 274); 'to become calm', *sakana*, 'to be quiet', (Bak, 418), *tmaskan*, 'to be improvised, unfortunate', (Ḥana, *Mu'jam*, II, 111); 'to abase o.s.', CA < *miskīn*, 'poor, (Sām, 191).

Marṭag, more commonly *tmṭrag*, 'to lie down', (Ḥana, *Mu'jam*, II, 112).

Masmar/basmagh, 'to nail' < *mismār* and *busmār*, 'a nail', (Sām, 154; Ḥana, *Mu'jam*, I, 523; Mac, I, 425), *tbasmar*, 'to be nailed to the spot'; (Mac, I, 432; YD, *Sefat*, 178).

Ma'yar, 'to blame' < *mi'yār*, 'shame'.

Maḥyal, *tmaḥyal*, 'to lie', 'to cheat' < *ḥīlah*, 'a lie', CA (Ḥana, *Mu'jam*, II, 109).

Maḥzar, (in Nāsiriyah), 'to stink', *miḥzīr*, 'unpleasant smell', (Ḥana, *al-Alfāẓ*, 94).

Madyan, *tmadyan*, 'to visit *al-madīnah*', i.e. Mecca, (Ḥana, *Mu'jam*, II, 109).

Mal'an, 'to make behave viciously', 'to toy', (Altomā, 59), *tmal'an*, 'to become sly, wicked', (Ḥana, *Mu'jam*, II, 113) < *mal'ūn*, 'cursed'.

Mar'ad, 'to cut into small pieces, *ra'ada*', 'to tear', (Sām, 181).

Markan, *maghkan*, 'to soak leather in a large *markan*' (basin), (Bak, 467).

Marshagh, *marshagh lah*, 'to gossip about others' bad attributes' < *mirshāg*, 'a piece of wood used by weavers', (an epithet for penis).

Médan, *tmédan*, 'to become a city dweller'< *madīnah*, 'city', (Ḥana, *Mu'jam*, II, 117); 'to run laps around a track' < Per, *midān*, 'track', (Shīr, 148; DH, *Qāmūs*, 277).

Naḥwar, *tnaḥwar*, 'to pronounce the grammatical cases of the words according to Arabic grammar', 'to brag', 'to enunciate carefully', used as an epithet (Shāl, II, 325).

Nashtar, 'to lance', 'to cut open', (Wood, 458) < Per, *nishtār*, 'a lancet' < Arm, *nésharah*, or *nésarah*; 'to sew', (YM I, *Hebrew-Aramaic*, 331).

Pargal, 'to be actively engaged in business', < Per. *purgal* (Cha, *Kalimāt* 30).

Parṭaḥ, bartakh, falṭaḥ, 'to flatten', 'to make broad', (Bak, 104; Cha, *Ath*, 24), Arm, *purṭākhā*, 'to widen a metal', *mparṭakh*, 'a wide face', or dissim. *faṭṭaḥa* where *ṭṭ* > *lṭ*.

Paswar, 'to become old, good for nothing', (Gīl, 205; Shāl, II, 41), 'to wither' (fruit, flowers), (Ḥana, *Mu'jam*, I, 694), *mpaswir*, 'out of order', (YD, *Sefat*, 248; Shāl, III, 41).

Pazman, 'to chant a *pizmōn*' (liturgical hymn) (Jews in Mosul), (Avīshūr, 227).

Pōdar, *tpōdar*, 'to apply powder', (Wood, 53; Ḥana, *Mu'jam*, I, 705).

Qalfaṭ, a distortion of *jalfaṭ*.

Qambar, *qampar*, 'to commit sodomy with boys' < *qurumpārah*, 'homosexual', (Wood, 371; MM, 248; Gīl, 220; YD, *Sefat*, 197).

Qamṭar, 'to swaddle' (a baby), 'to bandage' < CA, *qamaṭa*, or *qammaṭa*, 'same'.

Qandar, 'to hit with a shoe', 'to humiliate' (fig.), *kundura*, Tur, 'shoe'.

Qanfadh and *ganfadh*, 'to sit like a *qunfudh* (hedgehog) due to cold', (Cha, *Ath*, 79; Thin, 179). This verb is attested in the Kuwaiti dialect, (Ḥana, *al-Alfāẓ*, 320).

Qarmaz, ('Awwād, 24), 'to make s.th. dark red'; to become crimson', (Shīr, 125; TA, 58), Per, *qirmiz*, 'red'.

Qasṭal, 'to murmur' (river), (Ch, *Ath*, 71), *qasṭalah*, 'murmuring', CA.

Qōfal, 'to lock' < *qifil*, 'locker' or < *qafala*, 'to lock'.

Qōlaj, 'to have a stomach ache' < *qōlanj*, an internal disease, (*Muḥīṭ*, 732; DH, *Qāmūs*, 228), 'stomach ache due to inflammation of the large intestine', (YD, *Sefat*, 54), Per. *qōlāj*. The literal meaning of *qōlanj*, is 'a wind that causes pain in the stomach' (AN, 143).

Ka'bar, 'to crumple', (Wood, 407), 'to do a job carelessly'; (Sām, 179) < *ku'būrrah*, 'leftover food'; 'to roll into a ball shape', (Thin, 145). It may also be a composition of *kabura* and *ka'aba*, or *ka'war* > *ka'bar*, *w* > *b*.

Randaj, 'to plane'; (Ḥana, *Mu'jam*, III, 207; Thin, 86; Sām, 188; TA, 93; YM I, *Hebrew-Aramaic*, 301; Mac, I, 425; Cha, *Kalimāt*, 93) < *rendeh*; Per, 'a carpenter's plane'; Arm, *mérandōshéh*, 'to polish, smooth'.

Rastaq, or < *razdaq*, 'to arrange in order like the beads of a rosary', Syr, (*rōsqā*), (FM 196), 'to settle matters and establish order', (DH, *Qāmūs*, 122) < Per, *rasteh*, 'order'.

Réshan and *rayshan*, 'to grow feathers' (*rīsh*), and figuratively, 'to become rich', (Ḥana, *Mu'jam*, 222).

Sabdaj, 'to apply *sibdāj/isbīdāj* (a cosmetic powder) to the face', (Thin, 96), 'to scrub one's face with ceruse (a skin-whitening cosmetic)', (Wood, 211), Tur, *séfidaj*, and Per, *safīdrang* or *aspīdāj*, (Cha, *Kalimāt*, 8; TA, 2; Bak, 261; Baz, 96).

Ṣafraj, 'to become yellowish'< *ṣafrash* < *aṣfar*, 'yellow', (Sām, 169). The suffix *sh* in *ṣafrash*, denotes 'a small amount'.

Ṣafran, 'to become pale, faint, or yellowish', (DH, *Qāmūs*, 141).

Ṣāghlam, *ṣalgham*, 'safe and sound', 'whole, in one piece', 'to be in perfect condition'< Tur, *ṣāgh salīm*, 'same', ('Awwād, 24; Thin, 66; Wood, 265; MM, 218; Baz, 113). This verb is attested in the Kuwaiti dialect as *ṣalgham*, 'same', (Ḥana, *al-Alfāẓ*, 178).

Ṣahyan, 'to make s.o. a Zionist' < *Ziyyōn'*, Heb, 'Zion', *tṣahyan*, 'to become a Zionist'.

Ṣakhman, 'to sully', (Thin, 192; Bak, 441); 'to blacken with soot', (Mac, I, 421) < *sakhkham*, 'same', dissim. *-khkh* - > *-kh-km* (Sām, 166), < *sikhām*, 'soot', *s* > *ṣ* before *kh*). The *n* is a suffix. The expression *mṣakhkham mlaṭṭam* refers to someone whose face is blackened and is then beaten in the street as punishment (in the Middle Ages), (Shāl, III, 82).

Ṣakhraj, 'to become like a rock' < *ṣakhrah*, 'a rock'. The *j* is a suffix (Sām, 190), *tṣakhraj*, 'to be over-fried' (bricks), (Wood, 259).

Ṣakhtan, 'to be like fabricated merchandise'; 'to bluff', (Sām, 189; MM, 304) < *sikhtah*, 'a fabricated lie', (Gīl, 112).

Saktar, 'to expel, send away', (Sām, 65; Bak, 270); OTur, *siktirmek*, 'same'.

Ṣal'am, 'to make bald' < *aṣla'*, 'hairless', (Sām, 169).

Ṣalbakh, 'to calcify', 'to make bald'. This verb is attested in the dialects of the Gulf countries, (Qaf, 385) < *ṣalbūkh*, (Sām, 189), 'a small pebble', 'a hard stone'; Wood, 268), *mṣalbakh*, 'epithet of a person who shaved his hair entirely', (Ḥana, *al-Alfāẓ*, 222).

Salham, 'to close one's eyelids languidly', (Sām, 166; al-Karmilī, II, *Majmū'ah*, II, 116, n. 10); 'to be changed' (colour) < CA, *islahamma*, 'same'.

Ṣalṭān, 'to install a ruler'< *sulṭān*, 'a ruler', Arm, *shōlṭānā*, (Baz, 78; Sām, 165).

Samsar, 'to act as a *simsār*' (a broker; a middle man), (Shīr, 91).

Sangar, *zanqar*, *zangar* (Turj, 41), 'to become angry', 'to stare', 'to look angrily', Per, *zankīrah*, (Bak, 254; DH, *Qāmūs*, 133; Sām, 166).

Sarbal, *sarwal*, *sharwal*, 'to clothe s.o. with baggy trousers', *sirbāl*, Arm *surbālā* (Soko, 829; FM, 279), *tsarbal*, 'to wear a *sirbāl*', Per, *shalvār*, Tur, *sarvar* (Thin, 56). However, if *sarbal* is derived from the Arabic stem √ SBL, the meaning of this verb is 'to hinder', 'to be an obstacle to others'.

Sargad, 'to talk a lot', as in *akhadhnā sargadah bilḥaçī*, 'he made us listen to his long story' < *sergedah*, Per, 'prattling'.

Ségaj, 'to coat with sesame seed oil', (Gīl, 120; Bak, 276) < *sīghaj*, 'sesame oil', *mséghij*, 'stained or coated with sesame oil', (YD, *Sefat*, 212).

Sōdan, 'to drive insane'; *tsōdan*, 'to go crazy', 'become depressed', (Wood, 229; Bak 121; al-Karmilī, *Majmū'ah*, I, 119) < *aswad*, 'black'.

Sōlaf, 'to tell stories' (of the past) < *salaf*, 'precedents', (FJ, 155); 'to reminisce', (Ḥajj, V, 353; Wood, 230) < *sālūfah*, 'a tale', (Dabb, 43).

Sanbal, 'to grow' (bushels of wheat) < *sinbilah*, 'a bushel', CA (Sām, 189).

Ṣonaj, ('Awwad, 24) 'to play the castanets', *ṣinjah*, 'castanets'.

Shalfaṭ, 'to be ulcerated', (Bak, 298), 'to have pimples'; Arm, *shulpahtā*, 'a pimple', (Cha, *Ath*, 59).

Shangaṣ, 'to support (a wall or paving', (MM, 21 2) < Per, *shīgāsh*, 'a piece of iron used to prepare the ground for paving'.

Shandakh, 'to stick out (thread from a dress, or a branch from a tree)', (Gīl, 128); 'to grow tall and strong', ('Ubaydī, 49; MM, 212; Bak, 302) < *shindākh*, 'a tall tree branch (*shundūkh*)', 'a hanging thread from a dress', (YD, *Sefat*, 140), in CA, 'tall'.

Shaqban, *çaqban*, 'to carry a load in a *shaqabān*' (a large sack), Per, *çeqūn'*, (YD, *Sefat*, 195; Gīl, 14; Sām, 189; Bak, 290).

Sharmaṭ, *shaghmaṭ*, 'to act immorally', Syr, *sharmūṭah*, 'a whore', (FM, 276); 'to tear into pieces', CA, *sharraṭa*, 'same', dissim. *-rr-* > *rm-* (DH, *Qāmūs*, 153); 'to unstitch', 'to be loose' (a thread from a dress); *tsharmaṭ*, 'to be unstitched', (Cha, *Ath*, 57). It is likely that this verb is the Aramaic *mésōrmōṭéh*, 'to pluck', where *s* > *sh*, (YM I, *Hebrew-Aramaic*, 296).

Sharnaq, 'to inject' < Arm, *shalanqah*, IA, *çirinqah* or, *çrenqah*, 'injection', syringe', (Wood, 214; Gīl, 146); 'to weave a shelter' (worms), (TA, 94).

Sarwal, (Cha, *Ath*, 57), Per, *shalvar*, Heb, *sharwūl*, 'sleeve', Syr, *rbāl*; 'to be swollen'. Accordingly, the *sh* is a prefix (Gīl, 238; FM, 279); a compound of the Persian words *sar*, 'above' and *bāl*, 'stature', (TA, 34).

Shéraz, 'to sew a border around the edge of a garment', (Wood, 254).

Sharyas, *shéras*, 'to paste' or 'to glue' < *shrīs*, 'glue', (Wood, 239).

Shéṭan, *shayṭan*, 'to make s.o. obnoxiously clever or naughty', (Wood, 255); 'to inspire devilish behaviour', (Bak, 423), *tshéṭan*, 'to become a devil', (Mac, 436; Erwin, *A Short Reference*, 79) < *shīṭan*, 'devil'.

Shōdhar, *çodar*, and *çodhar*, 'to pitch a tent', (Wood, 88), 'to cover with a *çādor*' (Per, 'a cover', 'a tent'), Arm, *çadéra*, 'a tent', (TA, 42; BY, 18; Ḥana, *Mu'jam*, II, 310).

Shōlakh, 'to cook *kashk*' (a dish made from the leaves and stems of beets and turnip), (Mosul), *shlakh*, Arm, 'beets', (Bak, 295).

Shōqal, 'to check the weight' < Arm, *shāqūl*, 'a type of scale', (Cha, *Ath*, 54).

Shōshab, 'to veil', Arm, *shōshapā*, 'a veil', 'handkerchief', *tshōshab*, 'to be covered (head, neck and shoulders)', (Bak, 122; Ch, *Ath*, 26).

Sōbar, 'to [give] and take', Arm, *saybar*, 'to take', (Cha, *Ath*, 52), but in Mosul, 'to deal with', as in the expression *maḥḥad ysoburu*, 'no one deals with him', (Bak, 273).

Ṭam'an, *iṭma'an*, 'to assure', 'to calm s.o' √ ṬM'N (Erwin, *A Short Reference*, 80).

Ṭaḥmaj, 'to chisel or carve badly', (Thin, 79); *mṭaḥmaj*, 'fat and ugly', CA, 'ugly', (Sām, 170).

Talmadh, 'to become a student or apprentice', (Wood, 58), Syr, *talmīdā*, 'student'.

Ṭarbaṣ, 'to make water flow on the ground'; *barbaṣ*, CA, 'same', (Thin, 73); √ RBS, Arm, *rbāṣ*, (Cha, *Ath*, 46).

Ṭarbash, *ṭaghbash*, 'to wear a *ṭarbūsh*' (fez headdress), (Wood, 287); 'to quarrel', Syr, *ṭārbahshā* > *ṭarbash*, where *h* is omitted to facilitate the pronunciation (FM, 344), or < *ṭabbasha*, 'to splash water with one's feet', (Ḥana, *al-Amthāl*, 232), dissim. *bb-* > *-rb-* (the *r* is an infix); 'to wear a *ṭaghbūshī*' (shoe), (Bak, 323).

Ṭarfash, 'to become fat', 'to recover from sickness' < Arm, *ṭarpéshtā*, 'flabby dangling skin', (Cha, *Ath*, 63).

Ṭarsa', 'to run fast out of fear', (Shīr, 112) < Per, *tarsā*, 'coward'.

Ṭarṭash, ('Awwād, 24), 'to splash', CA, 'same'.

Tashran, 'to become swollen' (human skin), (Sām, 155), 'to be enflamed', (Wood, 57), 'to have a scratchy throat because of a cold', 'to become reddish because of a severe cold' < *tashrīn*, the months of November and December in which the weather in Baghdad is very cold (Sām, 155; Ḥana, *Mu'jam*, II, 67). In Lebanese, it means 'to feed cows with mulberry leaves', (AF, *Mu'jam*, 21).

Tathwar, *istathwar*, 'to act stupidly like a bull' (*thawr*).

Tḥémar, *istaḥmar*, *ḥamran* and *istajḥash*, 'to act like a *ḥimār* or *jaḥash*' (both words meaning 'young donkey') (Bak, 44; Erwin, *A Short Reference*, 80).

Tōfaq, 'to be successful' < *tawfīq*, 'success'.

Wandakh, 'to faint', (Sām, 183); 'to shake the buttocks' (slang), (Naqqāsh, *Nzūlah*, 165); 'to be disappointed', (Shāl, II, 294), *twandakh*, 'to become dizzy and faint', (Ḥana, *Mu'jam*, II, 139); *mwandakh*, 'one who is in a deep sleep', (Bak, 476).

Zablaq, 'to slip from the hand like a *zablūq*' (a kind of fish), (Bak, 237). In Kurdish, *zablūq* is used as an insult for a bald man, however, al-Ḥanafī derives this verb from, *zabaqa*, 'to slip'. The *l* is an infix (Ḥana, *Mu'jam*, III, 234).

Zanbagh, *zambar*, 'to feel a desire for sex' (Gīl. 106); 'to fly into a rage' as if one's jugular veins are swelled, used also in the sense of becoming inflated with pride < *zabbara*, (Sām, 164; Shīr, *Mu'jam*, 75), *tzanbar*, 'to be arrogant', (MM, 178), *mzanbar*, 'an epithet for one who is in dire poverty', (Ḥana, *Mu'jam*, III, 260).

Zampar, 'to be a 'womanizer', 'sinful', Tur, *zampara*, 'womanizer' or 'angry' (Per. Shīr, 79; Cha, *Kalimāt*, 103). Likewise, *zamb/par*, 'to be furious' < (FM, 225); 'to shout with rage'; 'to become red with rage', dissim. *zabbara*, *-bb-* > *-mb-* (Sām, 164). Some Jews and Christians say *zambagh* instead, as if one has been stung by a wasp (*zanmbūr*), (Ḥana, *Mu'jam*, III, 260; Cha, *Kalimāt*, 103); *zambar 'alā*, 'to have sexual desire and an erection' (Gīl, 106; YD, *Sefat*, 218).

Zandaq, *tzandaq*, 'to become a *zindīq*' (atheist), (Shīr, 81).

Zanhar, ('Awwād, 23) 'to look attentively', 'to look out for s.o.' < *zenhār*, Per, 'caution', 'protection', (Shīr, 5).

Zanjal, 'to chain', (Sām, 188; MM, 179; Ḥana, *Mu'jam*, III, 263) < *zanjīl*, CA or < *zanjīr*, Per, 'chain'.

Zanqaṭ, 'to get pimples'< IA, *zunguṭah*, 'a pimple', *zékthā* (Cha, *Ath*, 48; 'Ubaydī, 54).

Zanṭar/gh, 'to feel cold or frozen', (Shīr, *Mu'jam*, 79), 'to swell and become red with pimples', ('Ubaydī, 54; Bak, 253) < Arm, *zanṭā*, 'abscess', (Cha, *Ath*, 49), *zanṭar 'alā*, 'to speak rudely to s.o.', (Ḥana, *Mu'jam*, III, 261).

Zaqfal, 'to lock' (door) < *zuqfalah* or *ziqfalah*, 'locker', (MM, 178; Ḥana, *Mu'jam*, III, 251).

Zaqnab, 'to cause indigestion', (Mac, I, 421), 'to feed *zaqnabūt*' (bitter food). Note the Mongolian *ziqanapurt*, 'a poisonous beetle causing swelling of the stomach when eaten by donkeys', (Wood, 205; Bak, 245; Sām, 189), from which comes the verb *zaqnab*, 'to give such food with the hope that it will prove harmful'. The word is sometimes employed in a curse as in *inshallah samm w-zaqnabūt*, 'May God [make it] poison and harmful food', (Mac, I, 421). However, the verb may be a compound of Persian *ziq+nabūd*, (lit. 'may it not be food'), (Thin, 48, n. 8), as in, for example, the husband asking his wife *Yā marah, 'ashshétī-l- wulid?*, 'Wife! Have you given the kids [their] dinner?' The wife answers, 'Yes, *zaqnabithum*', 'I have given them indigestion', meaning that she is fed up with the children misbehaving, (Mac, I, 421).

Zardam, *zardab*, 'to turn yellow with fear', Per, *zard*, 'yellow', (Shīr, 5). In CA, 'to wring' (the throat) < Per, *sar*, 'head'+*dūm* = *zardūm*, 'throat'.

Zarnakh, 'to poison with *zarnīkh*' (poison), or *zannakha*, dissim. *-nn-* > *rn-*, (Ḥana, *Mu'jam*, III, 244).

Zébaq, 'to slip from the hand like *zi'baq*' (mercury), (Shīr, 74; Bak, 237).
Jalfaṭ, (Awwād 23) < *Jalbaṭ*, *b* > f, 'to become sticky', CA.
Zétan, 'to coat with oil', *zayt*, 'oil', 'to become like *zaytūn*' (olive oil)'.

References

al-ʿĀnī = al-ʿĀnī, Walīd. 'Aghānī Shaʿbiyyah min ʿĀnah', *al-Turāth al-Sha'bī* V (Baghdad 1975), 199–204

AF, 'al-Fiʿl' = Furayḥah, Anīs. 'al-Fiʿl al-Rubāʿī Aṣluhu wa-Nushū'uhu wa-Maʿānīhī', *al-Muqtaṭaf* (Egypt 1973), 183–91

AF, *Mu'jam* = Furayḥah, Anīs. *Mu'jam al-Alfāẓ al-'Āmmiyyah* (Beirut 1973)

Altoma = Altoma, Salih. *The Problem of Diglossia in Arabic: A Comparative Study* (Cambridge 1969)

AN = Nūr-al-Dīn, ʿAlī. *al-Ta'rīb wa-Āthāruhu fī al-'Arabiyyah wal-Fārisiyyah* (Cairo 1979)

Avīshūr = Avīshūr Y. *ha-'Ivrīt she-ba-'Arvīt ha-Yehūdīt: ha-Markīv ha-'Ivrī véha-Aramī ba-'Arvīt ha-Yehūdīt shél kehīlot yéhūday 'Irāk, Sūryah 'u-Mitzrāyim* (Jerusalem 2000–1)

ʿAwwād = ʿAwwād, Kūrkīs. *Ashtāt Lughawiyyah* (Beirut 1990)

Bak = al-Bakrī, Ḥāzim. *Dirāsāt fī al-Alfāẓ al-'Āmmiyyah al-Mawṣūliyyah* (Baghdad 1972)

Baz = Bazargān, Rifʿat. *Mu'jam al-Alfāẓ al-Dakhīlah fī al-Lahjah al-'Irāqiyyah* (Baghdad 2000)

Ben-Jacob, *Hebrew and Aramaic* = Ben-Yacob, A. *Hebrew and Aramaic in the Language of the Jews of Iraq* (Hebrew) (Jerusalem 1985)

Blanc, Haim, *Communal Dialects in Baghdad* (Cambridge 1964)

Cha, *Kalimāt* = al-Çalabī, Dawūd. *Kalimāt Fārisiyyah Must'amalah fī 'Āmmiyyat al-Mawṣul* (Baghdad 1960)

Cha, *Ath* = al-Çalabī, Dawūd. *al-'Āthār al-'Ārāmiyyah fī Lughat Mawṣul al-'Āmmiyyah* (Baghdad 1935)

al-Dabbāgh = al-Dabbāgh, ʿAbd al-Khāliq. *Mu'jam Amthāl al-Mawṣul* (Mosul 1956)

DH = Dammūs, Ḥalīm. *Qāmūs al-'Awām* (Damascus 1923)

Driver = Driver G.R. *A Grammar of Colloquial Arabic of Syria and Palestine* (London 1925)

Dul = al-Dulayshī, ʿAbd al-Laṭīf. *al-Al'āb al-Sha'biyyah fī al-Baṣra* (Baghdad 1968)

EB = Badawi, El Said et al. *Modern Written Arabic: A Comprehensive Grammar* (New York 2004)

Erwin, *A Short Reference* = Erwin, W.M. *A Short Reference Grammar of Iraqi Arabic* (Georgetown 2004)

FJ = Fischer W. and Jastro, O. *Handbuch der arabischen Dialecte* (Wiesbaden 1980)

FM = Mubāraka, Fāḍil. *Baqāyā al-'Ārāmiyyah fī Lughat Ahl Ṣadad al-Maḥkiyyah* (Aleppo 1990)

Ghanīmah = Ghanīmah, Yūsuf. 'al-Alfāẓ al-Ārāmiyyah fī al-Lughah al-ʿIrāqiyyah', *Lisān al-'Arab* IV (December 1926), 265–71

Ghulāmī = al-Ghulāmī, Muḥammad. *Kitāb al-Muraddad min al-Amthāl al-'Āmmiyyah al-Mawṣuliyyah* (Baghdad 1964)

Gīl = Swéry, Gīlah, and Rajwān, R. *Dictionary of Iraqi Judeo-Arabic Dialect* (Hebrew) (Jerusalem 1995)

Ḥajj = al-Ḥajjiyyah, ʿAzīz. *Baghdādiyāt*, I (Baghdad 1967); II (1968); III (1973); IV (1981); V (1983); VI (1991); VII (1999)

Ḥajj, *al-Amthāl* = al-Ḥajjiyyah, ʿAzīz. *al-Amthāl wal-Kināyāt fī Shi'r al-Mullah 'Abbūd al-Karkhī* (Baghdad 1986)

Ḥana = al-Ḥanafī, Jalāl al-Dīn. 'Fī Fiqh al-ʿĀmmiyyah al-Baghdādiyyah, al-Turāth al-Shaʿbī', VI (Baghdad 1975), 63–6

Ḥana, *al-Alfāẓ* = al-Ḥanafī, Jalāl al-Dīn. *Mu'jam al-Alfāẓ al-Kuwaytiyyah* (Baghdad 1964)

Ḥana, *Mu'jam* = al-Ḥanafī, Jalāl al-Dīn. *Mu'jam al-Lughah al-'Āmmiyyah al-'Irāqiyyah*, I (Baghdad 1978); II (Baghdad 1982); III (Baghdad 1993)

Ḥanẓal = Ḥanẓal, al-Fāliḥ. *al-Alfāẓ al-'Āmmiyyah fī Dawlat al-'Imārāt al-'Arabiyyah al-Muttaḥidah* (Abu Dhabi 1998)

Jawād = Jawād, Muṣṭafā. 'al-Lughah al-ʿĀmmiyyah al-ʿIrāqiyyah', *Lisān al-'Arab* (Baghdad, year 8, 1933), 115–17

al-Karkhī, *Dīwān* = al-Karkhī, ʿAbbūd. *Dīwān al-Karkhī* III (Baghdad 1967)

Kāmil, Murād. *Nash'at al-Fi'l al-Rubā'ī fī al-Lughāt al-Sāmiyyah al-Ḥayyah* (Cairo 1963)

al-Karmilī, *Majmū'ah* = al-Karmilī, Anastas Mārī. *Majmū'ah fī al-Aghānī al-'Irāqiyyah*, vols, I and II. Edited byAmīr al-Sāmarrā'ī (Baghdad 1999)

al-Karmilī, *Dīwān* = al-Karmilī, Anastas Mārī. *Dīwān al-Tiftāf, aw Ḥikāyāt Baghdādiyyah*[2] (Baghdad 2000)

Mac, I, II = MacCarthy R. and Raffouli, F. *Spoken Arabic of Baghdad*, I (Baghdad 1964); II (Baghdad 1967)

al-Mallāh, 'Nukāt' = al-Mallāh, M. 'Nukāt wa-Ghara'ib Lughawiyyah', *Lughat al-'Arab* 6 (Cairo 1928), 349–53

Mansoor, Jacob. *The Jewish Dialect of Baghdad* (Jerusalem 1991)

Masliyah = Masliyah, Sadok, 'The Folk Songs of Iraqi Children', *JSS* 55:2 (2010), 539–88

Mélaméd = Mélaméd, Ezra. *Aramaic-Hebrew-English Dictionary of the Babylonian Talmud* (in Hebrew) (Jerusalem 2005)

Mez = Mez, A. *Uber einige sekundare Verba im Arabischen, Orientalische Studien, Th. Noldeke*, I (Giessen 1906), 249–54

MM = Muḥammad, Majīd. *Majma' al-Mu'allafāt wal-Alfāẓ al-Ajnabiyyah fī al-Lughah al-'Irāqiyyah al-Dārijah* (Baghdad 1990)

Moscati = Moscato, Sabatino et al. *An Introduction to the Grammar of the Semitic Languages* (Wiesbaden 1980)

Muḥīṭ = al-Bustānī, Buṭrus. *Muḥīṭ al-Muḥīṭ* (Lebanon 1977)

al-Munjid = *al-Munjid fī al-Lughah* (Beirut 1998)

al-Muzhir = Jalal al-Din al-Suyūṭī, *al-Muzhir fī 'Ulūm al-Lughah wa-Anwā'uah*, Vol. II (Cairo 1971)

Naqqāsh, *Nzūlah* = Naqqāsh, S. *Nzūlah wkhīt al-shayṭān : riwāyah 'Irāqīyyah* (Jerusalem 1986)

O'Leary = O'Leary, D.D. *Comparative Grammar of the Semitic Languages* (London 1923)

Oussani = Oussani, Gabriel. 'The Arabic Dialect of Baghdad', *Journal of the American Oriental Society* 22 (1901), 97–114

Piamenta = Piamenta, Moshe. *A Dictionary of Post-Classical Arabic*, Vols. I–II (Leiden 1990)

Qad = Qaddūrī, Ḥusayn. *Lu'ab wa-Aghānī al-Aṭfāl al-Sha'biyyah fī al-'Irāq*, I (Baghdad 1968); II (Baghdad 1975); III (Baghdad 1988)

Qaf = Qafisheh, Hamdi. *Gulf Arabic-English Dictionary* (Chicago 1997)

Rabīn = Rabīn, Chaim. 'The Nature and Origin of the Shaf'el in Hebrew and Aramaic', *Erétz-Yisrael*, IX, W.F. Albright volume, 148–58 (Hebrew) (Jerusalem 1969)

Sām = al-Sāmurrā'ī, Ibrāhīm. *al-Fi'l Zamānuhu wa-Abniyatuhu* (Baghdad 1966)

Sām, *al-Dakhīl* = al-Sāmurrā'ī, Ibrāhīm. *al-Dakhīl fī al-Fārisiyyah wal-'Arabiyyah* (Lebanon 2001)

Sām, *al-Tawzī'* = al-Sāmurrā'ī, Ibrāhīm. *al-Tawzī' al-Lughawī al-Jughrāfī fī al-'Irāq* (Baghdad 1968)

Sapir = Sapir, Edward. *Language* (New York 1949)

Shāl = al-Shāljī, 'Abbūd. *Mawsū'at al-Kināyāt al-'Āmmiyyah al-Baghdādiyyah*, I (Baghdad 1979); II (Baghdad 1982); III (Baghdad 1983)

Shīr = Shīr, Addī. *Mu'jam al-Alfāẓ al-Fārisiyyah al-Mu'arrabah* (Beirut 1980)

Shūḥān = Shūḥān, Aḥmad. *al-Amthāl al-Furātiyyah* (Damascus 1984)

Soko = Sokoloff, Michael. *A Dictionary of Judeo Aramaic* (Ramat-Gan 2003)

Stein =. Steingass, F. *Comprehensive Persian-English Dictionary* (New Delhi 1996)

TA = al-ʿUnaysī, Ṭūbyā. *Kitāb al-Alfāẓ al-Dakhīlah fī al-Lughah al-'Arabiyyah* (Egypt 1932)

Thin = Thinyān, ʿAbd al-Laṭīf. *Ṣafaḥāt min Qāmūs al-'Awām fī Dār al-Salām* (Baghdad 2001)

Tikrītī = al-Tikrītī, ʿAbd al-Raḥmān. *Jamharat al-Amthāl al-Baghdādiyyah*, I (Baghdad 1971); V (1986); VI (1991)

Ṭobī = Ṭobī, Yoséf. 'ha-Peʿalīm ha-Merubaʿīm ba-ʿIvrīt ha-Meduberet shebéfi Yehuday Ṣanʿa', (Hebrew), *Masorot* II (1986), 65–78

Turj = Turjmān, ʿAbbās. *Malāmiḥ al-Lahjah al-Najafiyyah, 'Uṣūluhā wa-'Adabuhā* (Beirut 2002)

ʿUbaydī = al-ʿUbaydī, Azhar. *al-Mawṣul, Ayyām Zamān* (Mosul 1989)

Wehr = Wehr, Hans. *A Dictionary of Modern Written Arabic*. Edited by J. Milton Cowan (New York 1964)

Wood = Woodhead D. and Wayne, B. *A Dictionary of Iraqi Arabic, Arabic-English* (Washington 1967)

Wright = Wright, William. *A Grammar of the Arabic Language*[3] (Cambridge 1976)

Yahuda = Yahuda, Abraham Shalom Ezekiel. 'Bagdadische Sprichwörter' in *Orientalische Theodor Nöldeke* (Giessen 1906), 399–416

Yannay = Yannay, Igal. = 'The Quadriliteral Verbs in the Hebrew Language', Ph.D. dissertation (University of California, Los Angeles 1970)

YD, *Sefat* = Yoséf, Davīd. *Sefat ha'ém: Milon ha-Nistolgyah shél ha-'Iraqīm*, (Hebrew) (Jerusalem, n.d)

YM I, *Hebrew-Aramaic* = Yona, Mordechai. *Hebrew-Aramaic-Kurdish Dictionary* (Hebrew) (Jerusalem 1990)

YM II, *Aramaic-Kurdish* = Yona, Mordechai. *Aramaic-Kurdish–Hebrew Dictionary* (Hebrew) (Jerusalem 1990)